Nobel Laureates

The Secret

of Their Success

David Pratt

Branden Books,
Boston

Library of Congress Cataloging-in-Publication Data

Names: Pratt, David, 1939-
Title: Nobel laureates : the secret of their success / David Pratt.
Description: 1st edition. | Boston : Branden Books, 2016. | Includes
  bibliographical references and index.
Identifiers: LCCN 2016011222 (print) | LCCN 2016013215 (ebook) |
ISBN
  9780828326223 (paperback : alkaline paper) | ISBN 9780828326230
(e-book) |
  ISBN 9780828326230 (E-Book)
Subjects: LCSH: Nobel Prize winners--Biography--Anecdotes. |
Successful
  people--Biography--Anecdotes. | Nobel Prizes--History--Anecdotes. |
  Success--Anecdotes.
Classification: LCC AS911.N9 P74 2016 (print) | LCC AS911.N9
(ebook) | DDC
  920.02--dc23
LC record available at http://lccn.loc.gov/2016011222

Paperback ISBN 9780828326223
E-Book ISBN 9780828326230

Branden Books
PO box 812094
Wellesley MA 02482

brandenbooks.com

Contents

Preface

"People keep writing to ask me the meaning of life," complained Albert Einstein after he won the Nobel Prize for Physics in 1921. "What am I to tell them?" Since its inception in 1901, the prize has been viewed as the hallmark of genius, and the laureates as gurus whose views are sought on all subjects. There are other international prizes that are financially more valuable, but there is none that has greater prestige. The history of the Nobel Prize reflects the history of the twentieth and early twenty-first century, with prizes for medicine given for discoveries from insulin to organ transplants, and for peace for contributions to the Versailles Treaty and to the ending of the Cold War.

Another question laureates are frequently asked is: How do you win a Nobel Prize? One Nobel Prize winner, Michael Bishop (Medicine 1989), obliged with a book entitled, *How To Win The Nobel Prize*, and another, Peter Doherty (Medicine, 1996), wrote a book called *The Beginner's Guide to Winning the Nobel Prize*. Practical advice was offered by George Beadle (Medicine 1958). In response to a telegram of congratulation from his Caltech students, he replied: "You too can win Nobel Prizes. Study diligently. Respect DNA. Don't smoke. Don't drink. Avoid women and politics. That's my formula." Less forthcoming was Robert Laughlin (Physics 1998), who said, "If I knew what leads one to the Nobel Prize, I wouldn't tell you, but go get another one."

If the path to the Nobel Prize is uncertain, are there common factors among Nobel laureates that help to account for their achievements? Is their childhood privileged or challenging? Are they precocious as children? Are teachers important in their lives or are they self-taught? How significant is gender? Do Nobel Prize winners work in solitude or in collaboration? How important to their success are intelligence, persistence, creativity, and intuition? Is marital stability a factor? How many of them have experienced tragedy, or imprisonment, or exile, or war at first hand? Is eccentricity a necessary part of their genius? Has anyone ever refused the Nobel Prize? Do many laureates agree with Doris Lessing (Literature, 2007), who called the prize "a bloody disaster"? Who has been overlooked by the Nobel selectors? Collectively, the answers to these questions provide guideposts to the pathways to extraordinary achievement. But the secret of their success is something different.

Alfred Nobel was born in Sweden in 1833. He grew up in Russia, where his father was an explosives manufacturer, but he travelled widely, living for many years in France and the United States. Like his father, he engaged in manufacturing explosives, but he also made inventions in many other areas, taking out over 350 patents, including those for artificial silk and artificial leather. His major innovation was to find a way to make nitro-glycerin stable—an explosion had destroyed one of his factories and killed one of his brothers—by mixing it with inert substances to form dynamite. He believed that dynamite would be so powerful a weapon that it would make future wars unthinkable. Dynamite was rapidly adopted in the mining and construction industries, bringing huge wealth to Nobel.

Nobel was a lifelong bachelor, fluent in Swedish, Russian, French, English, and German. He wrote novels, plays, and poetry. Toward the end of his life, in 1895, he drew up his will. The will stipulated that the bulk of his fortune should be invested in a fund, and the annual interest should be divided in five equal parts, to be awarded one part to the person who shall have made the most important discovery or invention within the field of physics; one part to the person who shall have made the most important chemical discovery or improvement; one part to the person who shall have made the most important discovery within the domain of physiology or medicine; one part to the person who shall have produced in the field of literature the most outstanding work of an idealistic tendency; and one part to the person who shall have done the most or the best work for fraternity among nations, for the abolition or reduction of standing armies, and for the holding and promotion of peace congresses.

Each prize could be shared by a maximum of three persons. In 1969, a sixth prize was added, when the Bank of Sweden established the "Bank of Sweden Prize in Economic Sciences in Memory of Alfred Nobel." The names of the prizes are normally abbreviated to Chemistry, Economics, Literature, Medicine, Peace, and Physics.

The prizes are awarded by four institutions. The prizes in Physics, Chemistry, and Economics are awarded by the Royal Swedish Academy of Science. The Karolinska Institutet in Stockholm is responsible for the prize in medicine. The Swedish Academy is responsible for the prize in literature. And the peace prize is awarded by the Norwegian Parliament.

Each of these bodies establishes a committee that is responsible for naming the laureates. With the exception of the Swedish government's appointment of one auditor, the Nobel Foundation is completely independent of the government.

The first prizes were worth 150,000 Swedish kronor, which at the time was about 20 times the annual income of a Swedish professor. Nobel's intention was to free the laureate from the necessity of paid employment. The value of the prize did not alter much for many years, but in 1946 the Nobel Foundation was exempted from taxes, and in 1953 its investment rules were liberalized, resulting in rapid growth of its capital. The nominal fund capital of the Nobel Foundation was in 2011 about 3.1 billion Swedish kronor. In 2001-2011, the value of each prize was 10,000,000 Swedish kronor. As a result of market conditions, the value was decreased to 8,000,000 million SK in 2012, or $1,220,000. The laureate also receives an inscribed diploma and a gold medal. The medal is of gold, 2½ inches in diameter, and worth 20,000 Swedish kronor in 1991 values, its thickness varying with the price of gold.

Each year, the Nobel committees send out several hundred requests for nominations to eligible nominators. These include leading professors in the field, previous prize winners, and members of the committee. In the case of the Peace Prize, nominators include members of the Norwegian Parliament, and leading members of interparliamentary and interjudicial bodies. Nominators for the literature prize include members of the Swedish academy and similar bodies in other countries, and presidents of national writers' organizations. People may not nominate themselves for a prize. Nominations must be received by February 1 each year. From the nominations, which today typically number two to three hundred for each prize, the committee then produces a short list of names from which it selects one, two, or three laureates. The nominations and committee discussions are secret, and the files remain closed for fifty years. Names of the prize winners are announced in the first half of October. The prizes are always awarded on December 10, the anniversary of Alfred Nobel's death. The ceremonies, held with great pomp and dignity, in the presence of the royal family, are held in Oslo for the Peace Prize, and in Stockholm for the other prizes.

At the formal banquet on December 10, each prize winner makes a brief acceptance speech, or if the prize is shared one of the winners does so. In Stockholm, the banquet is held in the City Hall with 1300 guests.

Invitations to the banquet are eagerly sought. According to the Nobel Foundation:

> Occasionally a Laureate has invited both his ex-wife and his current wife to accompany him to Stockholm. On one such occasion, the Nobel Foundation received instructions to seat these ladies far apart, without any possibility of eye contact, and it followed these instructions, for the sake of domestic peace.

At the Nobel celebrations in 1979, Abdus Salam, the laureate in physics, arrived with his two wives, creating some problems of protocol.

Each laureate is also required to deliver a lecture, which is usually given during the few days before or after the prize ceremony. The events constitute a week-long party for the citizens of Oslo and Stockholm in the middle of the dark Scandinavian winter. On Lucia Day, December 13, the laureate is woken by a choir, led by a girl wearing a crown of lighted candles (followed by an aide carrying a damp towel in case of accidents). Many laureates have observed that the Nobel experience was for themselves and their families like living in a fairy tale.

In its first 114 years, the Nobel Prize was awarded to 889 individuals; in addition, 25 organizations received the Peace Prize. Four people have won two prizes: Marie Curie (Physics 1903 and Chemistry 1911), Linus Pauling (Chemistry 1954 and Peace 1962), Frederick Sanger (Chemistry 1958 and 1980), and John Bardeen (Physics 1956 and 1972). The Red Cross has been awarded the Peace Prize three times, and it has been given twice to the United Nations High Commission for Refugees.

Chapter 1
Unless You're Poor, You Don't Know What Poor Means

Each year, approximately one out of every 600 million people on earth wins a Nobel Prize. You are 600 times more likely to be struck by lightning than to win a Nobel Prize. By any measure, this achievement is extraordinary. The accomplishments that earn the prize—scientific, literary, or for peace—are often described as works of genius, though Nobel laureates themselves modestly disagree. Whatever the case, the lives of these exceptionally high achievers provide intriguing clues to the pathways to success.

Nobel laureates, like everyone else, are marked by experiences in childhood. But generalizations are elusive; there are no universal characteristics of family or background that are predictive of their success. The typical laureate is the offspring of a professional or academic family, growing up in the relative privilege of the middle class. But to this commonality there are many exceptions. A childhood spent in poverty is not a disqualification for a Nobel Prize. No case makes this clearer than that of Mario Capecchi.

Capecchi, who won the Nobel Prize for medicine in 2007, spent his childhood as an abandoned child on the streets of wartime Italy. In an interview, he described an episode from this period:

> I found shelter either in houses that were bombed out or in houses that were given up by other people. One of the places that we stayed was actually a house that the Germans were using for torturing people. When you went in there, all the body parts were just left there on the floor. So I saw all sorts of body parts that were just cut off: fingers, noses, ears, and so on. This would be between the ages of 5 and 8.

Mario's grandmother was an American from Oregon, a gifted artist who went to Italy in order to paint. His mother was a poet and linguist who had studied and lectured at the Sorbonne, and belonged to a group of anti-fascist poets. She fell in love with a pilot in the Italian Air Force, but decided not to marry him. Mario was born in Verona in 1937; his mother taught him to speak both Italian and German. Realizing that she would probably be arrested for her political views, she sold some of her possessions and gave the money to a farming family in the Tyrol to take care of the boy. She was arrested in 1941 and sent to a concentration camp. The farm workers were occasionally strafed in the fields by American planes, and on one occasion Mario received a bullet in the leg.

After a year the money disappeared, and the boy was put out on the streets. He traveled to the south. For brief periods he stayed with his father, but left on account of the latter's abusiveness. Periodically he was arrested by the police and placed in orphanages, from which he escaped. He was inducted into the *Balilla*, Mussolini's youth army, from which he also escaped after a month. Living on his wits, joining various gangs, Mario survived on what he could steal or scavenge.

The end of the war saw Mario in hospital living on starvation rations and suffering from malnutrition and typhoid. There, in October 1946, on his ninth birthday, his mother found him. She had survived the concentration camp, though aged and deeply scarred by her experiences. Mario had his first bath in six years. His mother's brother, a physicist living in the United States, who had been searching for his sister, sent the passage fare, and within weeks they were in America, living in a Quaker community near Philadelphia.

Mario went to school for the first time, unable to read or write, or to speak a word of English. He suffered such bad nightmares that sheets would be torn and the bed broken. The emotional support of the community helped him overcome his post-traumatic stress disorder. His uncle was his academic inspiration. he was a physicist at Princeton who had helped develop the first electron microscope. On graduation from high school, where Mario played football, soccer, and baseball and was a star of the wrestling team, he entered Antioch College, where he initially studied political science, hoping to combine his love of science with his sense of political responsibility. But finding little science in political science, he switched to physics and chemistry.

He went on to Harvard, where he specialized in molecular biology and where James Watson (Medicine, 1962) was his graduate advisor. He earned his Ph.D. in 1967 and in 1968 joined the biochemistry faculty at Harvard Medical School. In 1973, in search of more isolation to pursue his research, he moved to the University of Utah. There he developed techniques enabling researchers to mutate genes in mammalian cells, making it possible to generate mice with human diseases for analysis. In 2007, he was awarded the Nobel Prize in medicine, together with Martin Evans and Oliver Smithies, "for their discoveries of principles for introducing specific gene modifications in mice by the use of embryonic stem cells." He lives with his wife and daughter in a remote house in the mountains near Salt Lake City.

Of his early life, Capecchi says:

> I think I did learn certain important things in early life: mainly how to take care of myself and how to become self-sufficient. What I had to do when I was four and one-half years old was simply to survive. I think that many kids did not make it and their story is untold, but I was fortunate enough to survive the whole thing. So I look at all of that as a series of stochastic lucky breaks.

Mario Capecchi is not typical of Nobel laureates, but a number of laureates have grown up in straightened circumstances. One of these is Albert Camus, who won the Prize for Literature in 1957.

Camus was born in Algeria in 1913. His father was killed at the Battle of the Marne when Albert was less than one year old. His mother, whom Albert loved dearly, was overwhelmed by life and exhausted by her job as a cleaner; the household was ruled by his harsh and unsympathetic grandmother. Although very poor, Albert's early life was not unhappy. There was a group of school friends, football, at which he excelled, the beach and the harbor for swimming, and above all the sunshine. Later, Camus would write, "No one who lives in the sunlight makes a failure of his life." Above all, there was Louis Germain, his dedicated elementary school teacher, who gave extra help to boys who showed academic promise. For Albert, he became a substitute father. He persuaded Camus' grandmother to allow Albert to sit the entrance exam to the lycée, rather than become an apprentice which would have brought some money into the family.

Albert's rigorous 12-hour days at his secondary school were interrupted for a year by the onset of tuberculosis, which troubled him for the rest of his life. He eventually received a B.A. and M.A. in philosophy from the University of Algiers. He published his first book, a collection of essays, at the age of 22. He joined the Communist Party in

1934, but was quickly disillusioned and was eventually expelled from the Party. He was active in a theatre group, Theatre du Travail, and worked as a journalist for the *Alger-Republicain*. In 1940 he moved to Paris, but in 1942 illness forced him into a sanatorium in central France. In 1943 he joined the Resistance, becoming editor of the Resistance newspaper, *Combat*, which he founded with Jean-Paul Sartre (Literature, 1964).

In his writings, Camus manifested high standards of intellectual independence and public and personal morality. In 1942, he published his short novel, *The Stranger*. The protagonist, *Mersault*, is a man who is incapable of speaking or acting falsely. He shoots an Arab on the beach, and is condemned to death, as much for his refusal to bow to social conventions as for his crime. The novel, written in the hardboiled tradition of American crime fiction, was so widely misunderstood that Camus included an explanatory afterword in later editions. In 1947, his other best-known novel, *The Plague*, was published. An allegory of the German occupation of France, *The Plague* is set in a North African town that is quarantined due to an outbreak of plague. In the book, Camus summarized his own philosophy:

> All I maintain is that on this earth there are pestilences and there are victims, and it's up to us, so far as it is possible, not to join forces with the pestilences.

Camus was rejected by the Left for his repudiation of communist totalitarianism, and by the Right for his championship of a negotiated peace in Algeria.

In 1957, he was awarded the Nobel Prize for Literature. Camus died in January 1959, at the age of 45, when the car in which he was traveling, driven by the nephew of his publisher, left the road and collided with a tree. The cause of the accident is still debated, but excessive speed was most likely a factor.

After winning the Nobel Prize, Camus wrote to his old teacher, M. Germain, to thank him for his help at a critical time. Louis Germain wrote back, in a letter beginning, "Mon cher enfant, (My dear child)..."

The lives of Albert Camus and Mario Capecchi are classic tales of rags-to-riches. They match the concept of a Nobel Prize raising an individual to prominence after a childhood of deprivation and an adulthood of obscurity. Such stories are not unique. But they are atypical. More characteristic of Nobel Prize winners is what Harriet Zuckerman calls "accumulated advantage." The "Matthew effect" is another name for the same principle, from the passage in the Gospel of Matthew (25:29), "For unto every one that hath shall be given, and he shall have abundance. But from him that hath not shall be taken away even that which he hath."

The typical Nobel laureate is born in a western country into middle class privilege. Like 95 per cent of Nobel laureates, he is male. His father is a professional, manager, or academic. His family has the knowledge and resources to seek out a good school, where he performs excellently, and he proceeds to a good university. His grades enable him to attend an elite university for graduate work. His graduate teachers are leading figures in their field. He receives his doctoral degree before he is 25, is awarded a one or two year fellowship by a foundation and undertakes post-doctoral work under a past or future Nobel laureate. Obtaining an academic position, usually in an elite university, he does his ground-breaking research in his late thirties or early forties, for which he is awarded the Nobel Prize fifteen years later. This is the standard pattern of life for a Nobel laureate in the sciences and economics. The pattern applies less accurately to laureates in literature and peace.

Clearly a privileged childhood may be helpful, but is not essential to later achievement. It will be noted, however, that in both the case of Camus and that of Capecchi, a mentor intervened at a crucial moment; in Camus' case, M. Germain made it possible for him to go to the lycée, and in that of Capecchi, his uncle brought him from Italy to the United States and then acted as a role model. We will have more to say about mentors at a later point.

Another laureate whose hard life began in childhood and continued into adulthood was Harry Martinson, a Swede who won the Nobel Prize for literature in 1974. His youth was marked by poverty and deprivation. He was born in 1904 in southern Sweden. His father, a heavy drinker, died of tuberculosis when the boy was six years old. In an action that would leave deep emotional scars, Harry's mother then abandoned him and his six sisters and went to the United States. The children were placed in foster care with local farmers. Over the next several years, Harry frequently ran away from the foster homes and orphanages in which he had been placed. At the age of 16, he became a sailor, and for the next seven years he worked as a ship's fireman. In breaks from the sea, he lived for a time in India, cut sugar cane in Brazil, took other laboring jobs, or became a vagrant. This is how he later referred to these years in his book Cape Farewell:

> Why do my thoughts turn so readily to stoke-holds? Perhaps because my life began there—there lie the years of my youth: dreamy hard-fisted years that stood their watch backwards across the seas; the years when muscles in the upper arm and the solar plexus grew and hardened in the endless shovel-play.

Periodically he resorted to begging. In 1927 he fell ill with tuberculosis and settled in Sweden, spending several periods in sanatoria. His first collection of poems was published in 1929. There followed several autobiographical novels. In 1934 he attended a writers' conference in the Soviet Union, and returned disillusioned. When the Russians invaded Finland in 1939, he enlisted in the Swedish Volunteer Corps and took part in the Winter War of 1939-40.

In 1949, Martinson became the first self-educated working class writer to be elected to the Swedish Academy. Negative criticism depressed him deeply, leading on one occasion to a suicide attempt. However, he continued to write poetry and plays. In 1974, he was awarded the Nobel Prize for Literature "for writings that catch the dewdrop and reflect the cosmos". He died in 1978.

Another Nobel laureate on whom poverty left its mark was Arno Penzias (Physics, 1978):

> Unless you're poor, you don't know what poor means. It means you get up in the morning and start killing cockroaches in the bathtub. It means wearing old clothes that make the other kids laugh at you. It means not being able to eat peaches until the end of August... To this day, I still feel different. It still hurts a little. Maybe that's why I work so hard for acceptance. I don't like Polish jokes. I don't like people who tease other people. I don't like anything that makes people feel badly about themselves.

While the norm for Nobel laureates is a privileged background, a childhood of poverty clearly does not preclude the possibility of a Nobel Prize.

Chapter 2
Cultural Capital

Is a privileged background necessary for success in life?

From a variety of sources it was possible to identify the occupations of fathers of 90 per cent of Nobel laureates up to 2011. The leading occupations are shown in Table 1.

Table 1
Leading Occupations of Fathers of Nobel Laureates, 1901-2011

Professor*	75
Small business owner	68
Artisan, skilled worker	58
Businessman, merchant	57
Physician, dentist	55
Engineer	45
Teacher, educator	42
Lawyer, judge	40
Manufacturer, director	34
Farmer	33
Civil servant	33
Clergy	30
Unskilled worker	23
Military, naval officer	22

*includes 12 professors of medicine,
who would also normally be MDs.

It is easy to see the advantages of being born into an academic family. Aside from inherited ability, there is an intellectual ambience, the stimulation from family friends and relatives, and the help and guidance that parents can give to their children's academic careers, all these factors part of what the French sociologist Bourdieu called "cultural capital". In the educational research literature, social-economic status is known as one of the most robust predictors of academic performance. As Selcuk Sirin (2005) says:

> Family SES sets the stage for students' academic performance both by directly providing resources at home and by indirectly providing the social capital that is necessary to succeed in school. Family SES also helps to determine the kind of school and classroom environment to which the student has access.

Sirin crunched the statistics from all of the sound studies he could find that compared academic achievement and parental social status. Looking at parental income, occupation, and educational level, he found a correlation of about .30 with academic achievement. This is a modest relationship, and means that 91% of academic achievement is explained by other factors.

A. Rothenberg and G. Wyshak examined the family background of Nobel laureates in science and literature. They found few cases where offspring followed the identical career path of their fathers, but they concluded that parents often had "unfulfilled creative wishes" in the case of literature laureates, and "unfulfilled creative and scientific wishes" in the case of science laureates.

In some cases, the academic line runs back more than one generation. Maria Goeppert Mayer, who won the prize for physics in 1963, wrote that "On my father's side I am the seventh straight generation of university professors." But it may be noted that some 20% of the Nobel laureates came from a background of small business owners and skilled and unskilled workers.

Harriet Zuckerman examined family background of science laureates and scientists in general from 1901 to 1976. She found that while 28% of scientists came from the professional class, 54% of science laureates did so. In other words the science laureates were a socially elite group even among other scientists.

There are plenty of exceptions to these generalizations. Einstein's father was an electrician. The father of Mairead Corrigan (Peace, 1976) was a window cleaner. Rosalind Yalow's mother completed sixth grade, and her father fourth grade.

A particular kind of privilege occurs when there is a Nobel laureate in the family. The parents of Irene Joliot-Curie (Chemistry 1935) were Marie and Pierre Curie, who won the Prize for Physics in 1903; Marie

Curie went on to win the Prize for Chemistry in 1911. J. J. Thomson, the British physicist, won the Prize in 1906; his son G. P. Thomson won the same Prize in 1937. Niels Bohr won the Prize for Physics in 1922; his son won it in 1975. William Henry Braggshared the Prize for Physics with his son William Lawrence Bragg in 1915. Hans von Euler-Chelpin won the Prize for Chemistry in 1929; his son Ulf von Euler won the Prize for Physics in 1970. Karl Siegbahn and his son Kai won the Prize for Physics in 1924 and 1981 respectively. Gunnar Myrdal, the Swedish economist, won the Prize for Economics in 1974; in 1982 his wife, Alva Myrdal, won the Peace Prize for her work on disarmament. Subrahmanyan Chandrasekhar, who won the Prize for Physics in 1983, was nephew of Venkara Raman, who won the Physics Prize in 1930. Gerardus 't Hooft won the Nobel Prize for Medicine in 1999; his grand uncle was Fritz Zernike, who received the Nobel in Physics in 1953. Jan Tinbergen won the Economics Prize in 1969; his brother Nikolaas won the Medicine Prize in 1973.

The kind of parenting people receive is probably at least as important as their social class. Sheldon Glashow (Physics, 1979) spoke for many laureates when he said:

> While my parents never had the time or money to secure a university education themselves, they were adamant that their children should. In comfort and in love, we were taught the joys of knowledge and of work well done.

Similarly, Carl Wieman (Physics, 2001), said:

> Probably the most important thing my parents did to encourage me was to NOT get a television. We lived way out in the woods and once a week we would drive into town (nearly an hour away) to buy groceries. On those trips my parents always took us to the public library.

Chapter 3
Fatherless Children

There is a folkloric tradition that success in adult life is a response to a deficiency of some kind in childhood. One Nobel laureate, George Wald (Medicine, 1967), spoke specifically to this issue:

> What one really needs is not Nobel laureates but love. How do you think one gets to be a Nobel laureate? Wanting love, that's how. Wanting it so bad one works all the time and ends up a Nobel laureate. It's a consolation prize.

How many Nobel laureates grew up lacking love we do not know. But a distinct minority of Nobel laureates are known to have grown up without fathers. Mihaly Csikszentmihalyi, in his interviews with 91 highly creative people, including several Nobel laureates, found that some 30% of the males in his sample lost a parent before they were in their teens.

Two mothers of Nobel laureates refused to marry the fathers: Mario Capecchi's mother, as we have seen, was one, the other was the mother of Willy Brandt, the German politician who won the Peace Prize in 1971. At least 40 Nobel laureates lost their fathers before the age of eleven, about double the normal rate.

The father of Aleksandr Solzhenitsyn (Literature 1970) died before his son was born. So did the father of Bertha von Suttner (Peace, 1905), and John Northrop (Chemistry 1946). Some have theorized that the loss or absence of a father acts as a stimulus to achievement. Jean-Paul Sartre's father died when Sartre was a boy. Had he lived, Sartre believed, "he would have crushed me. As luck had it, he died young." We can probably say that the success of these laureates is a tribute to the energy and devotion of their mothers.

The connection between early parental loss and adult psychopathology has been investigated by many researchers. While a number of studies have shown a link between childhood loss of father and adult depression, summaries of research have failed to do so. In one such study, Christopher Tennant concluded that, "If potential confounding variables are taken into account, there is a nonexistent or negligible long-term psychopathologic effect." The relationship between scientific genius and the loss of a parent was investigated by W. R. Woodward, who found no statistically significant results. Anecdotally, it is remarkable how many famous scientists lost a parent in childhood: Copernicus, Newton, Leibniz, von Humboldt, and Eddington lost fathers; Pascal, Boyle, Huyghens, Cavendish, Priestley, Lavoisier, Kelvin, and Maxwell lost mothers.

It may be that the death of a father is less important than the relationship between father and child. Bernice Eiduson studied forty research scientists and found "One striking finding stands out immediately: nineteen of the 40 scientists (47.5 per cent) did not know their fathers very well." S. M. Silverman reports that this line of research brings out clearly that a basic characteristic of the physical scientist is a fear of, and avoidance of, interpersonal (that is, human) contacts, and a replacement of these for the greater certainty and impersonality of physical law.

Paul Greengard (Medicine, 2000) made a similar point:

> A lot of the most talented people in science and other fields were very driven to do something with their lives and the reason that they were driven to do something with their lives had to do with childhood experiences that raised serious doubts in their minds as to their own inherent value... I'm always amazed at the remarkably high percentage of highly creative people who had very sad childhoods.

Fritz Haber, who could accurately be described as a workaholic, believed that "Work is the refuge of people who suffer materially and spiritually."

On the other hand, here is Richard Feynman (Physics, 1965) describing his father, who was a uniform salesman:

> We had the *Encyclopaedia Britannica* at home and even when I was a small boy [my father] used to sit me in his lap and read to me from the *Encyclopaedia Britannica*, and we would read, say, about dinosaurs and maybe it would be talking about the brontosaurus or something, or the tyrannosaurus rex, and it would say something like, "This things is twenty five feet high and the head is six feet across" you see, and so he'd stop all this to say, "Let's see what that means. That would mean that if he

stood in our front yard he would be high enough to put his head through the window…

We used to go the Catskill Mountains… When my father came he would take me for walks in the woods and tell me various interesting things that were going on in the woods… Looking at a bird he says "Do you know what that bird is? It's a brown throated thrush, but in Portuguese it's a… in Italian a…" he says, "in Chinese it's a… in Japanese a…" etcetera. "Now" he says, "you know in all the languages you want to know what the name of that bird is and when you're finished with all that," he says, "you'll know absolutely nothing whatever about the bird. You only know about humans in different places and what they call the bird. Now" he says, "Let's look at the bird."

Cesar Milstein (Medicine, 1984) had a similarly close relationship with his father, who, as an illiterate farm worker, had emigrated from Ukraine to the USA at fourteen. Milstein took his father to Jerusalem when he was awarded the Wolf Prize in 1980. In his speech of thanks in the Knesset, Milstein acknowledged the debt he owed to the support of his parents:

At this point, he [his father] jumped from his seat, came to the rostrom, and to my great embarrassment, gave me a kiss! The audience, however, loved it!

It would seem that Nobel laureates as a group survive absent fathers, suffer from emotionally distant fathers, and benefit from engaged fathers.

Chapter 4
A Well Educated Group

It is a logical question to ask how far education contributes to lifetime success. It will surprise no one that Nobel laureates are a well educated group. In Chemistry, Medicine, Physics and Economics, more than 90% of laureates had an earned doctorate (Ph.D., D.Phil., or M.D.). On the other hand, 47% of literature Nobels and 33% of Peace laureates had no degree. We are dealing here with somewhat different populations. In the sciences, formal education, normally including the doctorate, is a prerequisite to a career as a scientist.

The great majority of Nobel laureates do well at school, but there are exceptions. At the age of 15, when he was at Eton, John Gurdon (Medicine 2012) came 250th out of 250 pupils in science, and was told that his scientific ambitions were "ridiculous" and "a waste of time." Einstein was only an average pupil at school and dropped out when he was 15. He failed his entry examination to university on the first attempt and had to study for an additional year before he was successful. His grades in university were mediocre, and instead of pursuing an academic career he entered the Swiss Patent Office:

Winston Churchill (Literature, 1953) hated his school years.

> Nearly twelve years of school… form not only the least agreeable, but the only barren and unhappy period of my life… a time of discomfort, restriction and purposeless monotony… I would far rather have been apprenticed as a bricklayer's mate, or run errands as a messenger boy, or helped my father to dress the front windows of a grocer's shop. It would have been real; it would have been natural; it would have taught me more; and I should have done it much better.

Many Nobel laureates, on the other hand, express gratitude to the institutions they attended. Lee Hartwell (Medicine, 2001) observed that "I don't think I would have ever gotten the opportunity to spend my career in science if it hadn't been for a few key teachers along the way."

"It was Cambridge that made me, and I am forever grateful," said Max Perutz (Chemistry, 1962).

One Nobel scientist who missed obtaining a doctorate was Gertrude Elion (Medicine, 1988). She took her bachelor's degree at Hunter College and her master's at New York University. She obtained a position in the laboratory of George Hitchings, with whom she would later share the Nobel Prize. At the same time, she was studying part time for the Ph.D. at Brooklyn Polytechnic Institute. However, the Institute decided that Elion should attend full-time, which would entail her giving up her laboratory job. She elected to leave her doctoral work unfinished. After she won the Nobel Prize, Brooklyn Polytechnic gave her an honorary doctorate.

The Nobel Foundation publishes a list of universities with which Nobel laureates were affiliated at the time of their prize. The ten leading universities are shown in Table 2.

Table 2
Leading Universities of Nobel Laureates, 1902-2014

Harvard	34
Cambridge UK	27
Stanford	20
Berkeley	8
Caltech	17
MIT	17
Chicago	17
Columbia	16
Princeton	12
Rockefeller	11

Collectively, all the institutions of the University of California claim 62 Nobel prizes; the various universities and Ecoles Supérieures of Paris count 25. Twelve graduates of the City University of New York had obtained Nobel Prizes by 2014, the most of any public university, and a number of laureates have asserted that it was the college's free tuition that made university possible for them. The Nobel Foundation's criteria are somewhat restrictive. Cambridge University would come in at first place if we counted 65 graduates who became laureates, 59 laureates who at some time were members of the faculty, and 14 laureates who attended or conducted research at the university.

Would potential Nobel laureates have had the same success if they had attended mediocre universities? For scientists at least, the answer is: probably not in all cases. The elite undergraduate school is a stepping stone to an elite graduate school and thence to post-doctoral work at a significant science center. Nevertheless, there are sufficient Nobel Prize winners who have done their undergraduate and even graduate work at little-known universities to defy generalization.

Given their education and intellectual gifts, validated by the Nobel Prize, it is not surprising that journalists and the public treat them as oracles. Echoing Einstein, David Baltimore (Medicine, 1975) wrote that "People keep e-mailing me to ask: What is the meaning of life? And they want me to e-mail them back quickly with an answer!" Nobel laureates are expected to be omniscient, but they do not have an unblemished record when they endeavor to predict the future. Svante Arrhenius (Chemistry, 1903) predicted global warming in 1908, but thought it would be a good thing:

> By the influence of the increasing percentage of carbonic acid [carbon dioxide] in the atmosphere, we may hope to enjoy ages with more equable and better climates, especially as regards the colder regions of the earth, ages when the earth will bring forth much more abundant crops than at present, for the benefit of rapidly propagating mankind.

Lord Rayleigh, who won the prize for Physics in 1904, said, "I have not the smallest molecule of faith in aerial navigation other than ballooning." This was in 1896, seven years before the Wright Brothers' first flight. Ten years before the first atomic bomb was exploded, Ernest Rutherford, a pioneer in nuclear physics, said, "The energy produced by breaking down of the atom is a poor kind of thing. Anyone who expects a source of power from transformation of these atoms is talking moonshine." And Edward Purcell, who won the prize for Physics in 1952 said, "All this stuff about traveling around the universe in space suits belongs back where it came from, on the cereal box." This was only a year before Major Yuri Gagarin made the first manned space flight.

Leon Lederman (Physics, 1988) spoke for many laureates when he commented on the public's expectation of omniscience. Speaking of the prize, he said:

> It really has an aura about it. First of all, you become an expert on everything. You get interviewed. "What do you think about the Brazilian debt, or social security, or women's dresses?" I had an opinion about that: as short as possible.

Chapter 5
Hitler's Gift

The Nobel Prize is a Western institution. Ten countries hold 80% of all Nobel Prizes, but have only 11% of world population. Nobel laureates are concentrated in Europe, the United States, and Japan, with Africa and South America seriously underrepresented.

Table 3 shows the nationality of Nobel Prize winners up to 2012.

Table 3
Nationality of Nobel laureates, 1901-2014

United States	339
United Kingdom	110
Germany	82
France	59
Sweden	30
Switzerland	22
Russia/USSR	19
Japan	19
Italy	14
Netherlands	14
Denmark	14
Other countries	134

Ninety-six of the laureates associated with the United States in the 20th century were also claimed by other countries on grounds of birth or citizenship. In other words, there is a migration inflow or "brain drain" of future Nobel laureates from other countries to the United States.

The major shift in nationality of Nobel Prize winners during the 20th century was in the position of Germany. In the first two decades of the century, Germany was the leading recipient of Nobel Prizes, taking 24% of the total, while the United States received only 5%. In the last two decades of the century, Germany received 8%, while the United States received 51%.

This change was principally due to the racial policies of Nazi Germany. In April 1933, less than three months after the Nazis came to power, a law was passed for "the reconstruction of the civil service". Under this law, no one of "Non-Aryan descent" could work in the civil service. As the universities in Germany were state-run, this ruling applied to university professors. An exception was made for individuals who had served in the First World War, but this exception was later closed by the 1935 Nuremberg laws. The consequences for the universities were dire. Within a year, some 2600 scientists and scholars left Germany, the great majority going to Britain. German universities lost a quarter of their physicists. Seven of the refugees to Britain were Nobel laureates; another twenty won the Nobel Prize after emigrating. A book on the subject of the scientific emigration of German scientists to Britain and the US by Jean Medawar and David Pyke is entitled *Hitler's Gift*.

Max Planck (Physics, 1918) recognized the harm that this was doing to German science, and obtained an appointment with Hitler to discuss the matter in May:

> I then remarked that we were inflicting damage on ourselves by forcing Jews whose talents we needed to emigrate and that their talents would now be used for the benefit of foreigners. This he [Hitler] did not accept at all and held forth at great length about quite general matters, ending up by saying: "It is said that I suffer on occasion from weak nerves. That is a slander. I have nerves of steel." With that, he slapped his knee with great force, spoke more and more rapidly and began to shake with such uncontrollable rage that there was nothing I could do but keep silent and take my leave as soon as I decently could.

We can never know how many future or potential Nobel laureates perished in the Holocaust. We know more about those who escaped. Max Perutz (Chemistry, 1962) was one of these. Perutz was born in Vienna in 1914, into a family of textile manufacturers. His interest in science was awakened by one of his school teachers, and he took a degree in chemistry at the University of Vienna. He then moved to Cambridge in 1936, to undertake doctoral studies in the structure of hemoglobin at the

Cavendish Laboratory. His parents' business was expropriated by the Nazis, but Max was successful in getting them to Britain in 1939. In 1940, shortly after earning his doctorate, and in spite of his anti-Nazi credentials, he was interned as an enemy alien. He was held in various makeshift camps in Britain and then shipped to an internment camp in Canada. Of this event, he wrote:

> To have been arrested, interned and deported as an enemy alien by the English, whom I regarded as my friends, made me more bitter than to have lost freedom itself. Having first been rejected as a Jew by my native Austria, which I loved, I now found myself rejected as a German by my adopted country.

Perutz and his fellow internees were frequently treated as dangerous criminals, jeered at by troops and crowds they passed; on the voyage to Canada, the commanding officer referred to them as the "scum of the earth." Conditions were crowded on board and many men caught dysentery, including Perutz. In Canada, their situation improved somewhat when they were classified as Prisoners of War. The men were held in a camp above the St. Lawrence at Quebec, locked in at night 100 to a hut, guarded by day by machine guns and barbed wire. For a minor infraction, Perutz was locked in a punishment cell in the local jail, where he slept on the floor and caught scabies. The prisoners, many of whom were scientists, organized university-level classes, Perutz teaching the principles of X-ray analysis of crystals.

Late in 1940, the order came for his release, and he returned to Cambridge in January 1941 and resumed his work on hemoglobin. Despite the privations of the previous year, Perutz seems to have harbored little bitterness. In 1943, he agreed to participate in a top-secret war project. His task was to design a floating island made of ice sufficiently robust to land heavy bombers. He found that by mixing ice with wood pulp, the product was as hard as concrete. In a demonstration to senior officers, Lord Louis Mountbatten, Chief of Combined Operations, fired his revolver at a block of reinforced ice. The ice suffered little damage, but the bullet ricocheted, narrowly missing the marshal of the Royal Air Force, Viscount Portal. The scale of the proposed craft was enormous, and there were numerous technical problems. After the invasion of Europe, the military lost interest in the project, and it never went into production.

At the end of the war, Perutz returned to Cambridge. He suffered from gastric ailments almost all his life, but this did not prevent him from founding the Cambridge Laboratory of Molecular Biology, home of a dozen future Nobel laureates. From his youth a keen skier and mountaineer, he also became Britain's leading glaciologist, doing significant work on the crystal structure and flow mechanism of glaciers. An Antarctic glacier is named for him. He was awarded the Nobel Prize for Chemistry in 1962 for his X-ray diffraction analysis of the structure of hemoglobin. Throughout his life he remained modest and unimpressed by rank or age:

> This leads me to my final advice to young scientists. *Take no notice of what your elders tell you.* Since I have now become an elder myself, I shall leave it to a young logician to make what he can of the paradox.

As Planck, Haber, and many others realized, the persecution of the Jews was inflicting long term damage on the interests of Germany and Austria. Prior to 1933, approximately one third of Nobel scientists came from Germany. But between 1933 and 1960, Germany won only 8 Nobel Prizes.

Funds were set up by scientists to aid their Jewish colleagues, and organizations such as the Rockefeller Foundation came to their assistance. In 1965, Hans Krebs (Medicine 1953), speaking on behalf of ex-German refugees, presented a check to the Presidents of the Royal Society and the British Academy in gratitude for the welcome they had received in Britain. In his speech, he said:

> No sum of money can adequately and appropriately express our gratefulness to the British people. What this country of our adoption gave us was not just a new home and livelihood...'we also found a new and better way of life coming from an atmosphere of political oppression and persecution... We found a spirit of friendliness, humanity, tolerance and fairness. It is this way of life with which some of us, I for one, fell in love. We were given here a new home—not merely a shelter but a true home.

Another Jewish scientist lost to Germany by emigration was Walter Kohn (Chemistry, 1998). He was born in Vienna in 1923, in a middle class family. He received a good education at a gymnasium (academic high school), until he was expelled following the Anschluss, which united Germany and Austria. He then entered an excellent Jewish secondary school. In August 1939 he was able to escape to Britain. His parents stayed behind and perished. Like Max Perutz, Kohn was rounded up with other "enemy aliens" in 1940, held in various camps first in Britain and then in Canada. He was able to continue his education in the camps, thanks to interned scholars who taught courses to their fellow inmates. The twenty cents he earned per day as a lumberjack went toward the purchase of books on mathematics and science. In 1942 he was released from internment and was taken in by a family in Toronto. He gained admission to the University of Toronto, but interrupted his degree program in 1944 to enlist in the Canadian army. He was awarded a degree in applied mathematics in 1945, and immediately enrolled in graduate studies. After a master's degree at the University of Toronto, he moved on to Harvard, where his Ph.D. thesis was supervised by Julian Schwinger (Physics 1965). He did two years of postdoctoral research in Copenhagen, worked at Bell Laboratories, and then taught at the University of California, first at San Diego and subsequently at Santa Barbara. In 1998 he received the Nobel Prize for Chemistry "for his development of the density-functional theory". Reflecting on his life's work in an interview in 2001, he provided some insight into his motivation.

> A person, like myself, who… loses a lot of really close relatives somehow through accident or whatever, they automatically have a sense of carrying the lost relatives on his shoulders. I feel like I'm doing this work not only on my own behalf but on the behalf of people who didn't make it.

Chapter 6
Ways of Thinking
about the World

What role does religion play in the lives of Nobel laureates? Religion was a major factor in the emigration of thousands of scientists, including future Nobel Prize winners, from Nazi Germany. This is an appropriate point to examine the religious background of Nobel laureates.

The website JINFO.ORG analyzes the number of Jewish Nobel laureates up to 2012. It reports:

> At least 187 Jews and people of half- or three-quarters-Jewish ancestry have been awarded the Nobel Prize, accounting for 22% of all individual recipients worldwide between 1901 and 2012, and constituting 36% of all US recipients during the same period. In the research fields of Chemistry, Economics, Physics, and Physiology/Medicine, the corresponding world and US percentages are 27% and 39%, respectively. Among women laureates in the four research fields, the Jewish percentages (world and US) are 38% and 50%, respectively... Jews currently make up approximately 0.2% of the world's population and 2% of the US population.

The proportion of prizes won by Jewish laureates ranged from 41% for Economics to 9% for Peace. Commentators attribute the success of Jews in science and in academe to the Jewish cultural emphasis on scholarship and achievement, and the professional status of many Jewish families.

Harriet Zuckerman, writing in 1977, found that 1%, of US laureates in science, was Catholic. Louise Sherby identified 70 out of 720 laureates up to the year 2000 as Catholic, or 9.7% of the total. She identified 4 as Moslem, 4 as Hindu, and 1 as Buddhist.

Self-identified atheists, agnostics, and freethinkers account for 10.5% of Nobel laureates, but 35% of laureates in literature.

How important is religion in the lives of laureates? As might be expected, the range in attitudes is wide. Here is Richard Aumann, the Economics laureate for 2005:

> In science we have certain ways of thinking about the world, and in religion we have different ways of thinking about the world. Those two things coexist side by side without conflict.

Or Shmuel Agnon (Literature, 1966) in his Nobel acceptance speech:

> After all my possessions had been burned, God gave me the wisdom to return to Jerusalem. I returned to Jerusalem and it is by virtue of Jerusalem that I have written all that God has put into my heart and into my pen.

Albert Camus:

> I don't believe in God, that's true. But I am not an atheist nonetheless… I have a good deal of affection for the first Christian. I admire the way he lived, the way he died. My lack of imagination keeps me from following him any further.

Francis Crick (Medicine, 1962), co-discoverer of the double helix:

> Christianity may be OK between consenting adults in private but should not be taught to young children.

William Henry Bragg (Physics, 1915):

> From religion comes a man's purpose; from science, his power to achieve it. Sometimes people ask if religion and science are not opposed to one another. They are: in the sense that the thumb and fingers of my hand are opposed to one another. It is an opposition by means of which anything can be grasped.

Doris Lessing:

I am absolutely, childishly, allergic to religions—even though I have the greatest respect for our nature, which is profoundly religious.

Nadine Gordimer (Literature, 1991):

I'm an atheist. I wouldn't even call myself an agnostic. I am an atheist. But I think I have a basically religious temperament, perhaps even a profoundly religious one.

William Phillips (Physics, 1997):

Being an ordinary scientist and an ordinary Christian seems perfectly natural to me.

Christian Anfinsen (Chemistry, 1972):

I think only an idiot can be an atheist.

Pearl Buck (Literature, 1938):

I feel no need for any other faith than my faith in human beings. Like Confucius of old, I am so absorbed in the wonder of earth and the life upon it that I cannot think of heaven and angels.

Bertrand Russell (Literature, 1950):

My own view on religion is that of Lucretius. I regard it as a disease born of fear and as a source of untold misery to the human race.

Steven Weinberg (Physics, 1979):

One of the great achievements of science has been, if not to make it impossible for intelligent people to be religious, then at least to make it possible for them not to be religious.

For Einstein, his contemplation of the universe bordered on the religious:

A spirit is manifest in the laws of the universe, a spirit vastly superior to that of man and one in the face of which we with our modest powers must feel humble. In this way the pursuit of science leads to a religious feeling of a special sort.

The case of Alexis Carrel (Medicine, 1912) is of interest in this context. Carrel was born in Lyon, France, in 1873, the son of a businessman who died when Carrel was very young. He studied at the University of Lyon, took his medical degree there, and taught there prior to moving to the University of Chicago and then to the Rockefeller Institute for Medical Research. He worked on suturing techniques and on tissue and organ transplants. In 1912 he was awarded the Nobel Prize for medicine, "in recognition of his work on vascular suture and the transplantation of blood vessels and organs."

As a young doctor, Carrel made a journey to Lourdes. En route he shared a train compartment with a family taking their sick daughter to Lourdes in hope of a cure. The young woman was suffering from tubercular peritonitis. With the parents' permission, Carrel examined her and found her close to death. She had tubercular sores, lesions of the lungs, rapid and shallow breathing, and a severely distended abdomen. She was in great pain and could hardly speak. The young woman visited the Massabielle Grotto at Lourdes and Carrel saw her shortly thereafter. She was still lying on a stretcher, but her respiration and pulse were returning to normal. As he watched, the distention of her abdomen reduced and disappeared. She was pain-free and radiant. "I shall join the Sisters of St. Vincent de Paul, and nurse the sick," she announced. Carrel's conclusion was that:

> Certain facts observed in Lourdes cannot be accounted for by any of the known laws of wound healing and tissue regeneration. In the course of a miraculous cure, the rate of tissue construction greatly exceeds that which has ever been observed in the healing of a wound under optimum conditions... The cures seem to occur by the normal processes, but enormously accelerated.

Carrel's reputation was clouded toward the end of his life, when he accepted the directorship of the Alexis Carrel Foundation for the Study of Human Problems, set up by the Vichy Regime. He died in Paris in 1944.

What the Nobel laureates have in common is not a particular religious belief, but a faith in the work they are doing, whether it is science, literature, or the pursuit of peace and justice.

Chapter 7
We Think
You'd Be a Distracting Influence

Gender has historically been a factor in the award of Nobel Prizes. Table 4 shows the gender distribution for the different categories of prize.

Table 4
Men and Women Laureates, 1901-2014

Category	Total	Men	Women	% women
Physics	199	197	2	1.0
Chemistry	169	164	5	3.0
Medicine	207	194	13	6.3
Economics	75	73	2	2.7
Literature	111	97	14	12.6
Peace	103*	84	19	18.4
Total	864	817	47	5.3

*Does not include 25 organizations that received the Peace Prize

In its first 20 years (1901-1920), the Nobel Prize was awarded to 4 women (4.1%). In the last 20 years, (1994-2014), it was awarded to 20 (9.2%). The year 2009 set a record, with 5 of the 13 laureates being women. Also notable was the year 2011, in which three extraordinary women, Ellen Johnson Sirleaf and Leymah Gbowee of Liberia and Tawakkol Karman of Yemen, shared the Peace Prize.

To what extent is the gender imbalance the result of deliberate discrimination? Sharon Birtsch McGrayne has made a study of women Nobel laureates in science:

> Many of these women faced enormous obstacles. They were confined to basement laboratories and attic offices. They crawled behind furniture to attend science lectures. They worked in universities for decades without pay as volunteers—in the United

States as late as the 1970s. Science was supposed to be tough, rigorous and rational; women were supposed to be soft, weak, and irrational. As a consequence, women scientists were—by definition—unnatural beings.

At the beginning of the twentieth century, the position of women in universities was disadvantaged, particularly in Germany. In 1924, fewer than 10% of German university students were women; post-secondary education for women occurred mainly in the form of finishing schools. In France, despite her two Nobel Prizes and her professorship at the Sorbonne, Marie Curie was never elected to the French Academy of Sciences.

But the situation was not ideal for women in the United States, either. Barbara McClintock (Medicine, 1983) was treated so off-handedly by the University of Missouri that she abandoned the university environment and spent the rest of her career at the Cold Spring Harbor Laboratory on Long Island.

Gertrude Elion (Medicine, 1988) spoke of her experience trying to find a laboratory job in the Depression:

> Wherever I went—it was a Depression time, it was a time that there weren't many jobs to begin with, and what there were, they couldn't see any reason to take a woman. They would interview me for long periods of time, but then they would say, "Well, we think you'd be a distracting influence in the laboratory." Well, I guess I was kind of cute at the age of 19, but I can't imagine that I would have been a distracting influence.

Carl Cori (Medicine, 1947) became a full professor at Washington University in St. Louis at the age of 35; his wife and collaborator Gerty (Medicine, 1947) stayed at the rank of research associate for 13 years. It was only a wartime shortage of scientists that led to her appointment as associate professor in 1944. The Coris shared the Nobel Prize in 1947.

Maria Goeppert Mayer (Physics, 1963) worked for years as a "voluntary professor" at the University of Chicago; her husband was a professor there, and anti-nepotism rules prevented the university employing both a husband and wife. Only at the age of 53, ten years after completing the work that later won the couple the Nobel Prize, did she obtain a regular, full-time, paid university position.

In some cases, deserving women were overlooked for the Nobel Prize. Lise Meitner did much of the work on nuclear fission for which Otto Hahn (Physics 1944) received the prize. Jocelyn Bell Burnell probably should have shared the prize with Anthony Hewish (Physics 1974); it was she who discovered pulsars for which he was honored.

Rosalyn Yalow (Medicine, 1977) said:

> Women, even now, must exert more effort than men do for the same degree of success... The trouble with discrimination is not discrimination per se but rather that the people who are discriminated against think of themselves as second-class.

When she was asked what she planned to do with the Nobel Prize money, Yalow said:

> I can't think of anything in the world that I would want that I haven't had... I have my marriage, two wonderful children. I have a laboratory that is an absolute joy. I have energy. I have health. As long there is anything to be done, I am never tired.

When Dorothy Hodgkin (Medicine, 1963) was asked whether being a woman had hindered her career, she replied: "As a matter of fact, men were always particularly nice and helpful to me because I was a woman."

While matters may have improved, there is a long way to go to real equality. In American universities in 2002, women accounted for only 35% of tenured faculty members, and only 15% in science and engineering faculties. In 2004, women faculty was still outnumbered by men even in disciplines where they earned more Ph.D. than men. A government and private study, in 2006, made similar findings:

> Compared with men, women faculty members are generally paid less and promoted more slowly, receive fewer honors, and hold fewer leadership positions. These discrepancies do not appear to be based on productivity, the significance of their work, or any other performance measures.

The report went on to point out that women have earned more than half of the bachelor's degrees awarded in science and engineering since

2000, yet among those with a science or engineering Ph.D. four times more men than women hold full-time faculty positions.

If there is a problem with recruitment to university positions, it is not the only one. It is still widely believed that girls perform less well than boys in mathematics, despite convincing evidence to the contrary, and this may affect those who teach and advise them. But it is in graduate school and the early years in the professoriate that women most suffer "cumulative disadvantage." As one study reports:

> In graduate school, behaviour is expected to be independent, strategic and void of interpersonal support. These expectations are antithetical to traditional female socialization… Essentially women are expected to follow a "male model" of academic success involving a total time commitment to scientific work and aggressive competitive relations with peers.

Women report either being invisible to male faculty or being given excessive visibility. Particularly problematic is the conflict between the graduate student role and child bearing. A female faculty member stated that:

> If a student had a baby with her, I wouldn't have her. Students who have babies here get no work done. It's not that I wouldn't take a woman with a child in the first place, but the first sign of trouble, I would just tell them to go away. If my students fail it looks bad for me.

The years leading up to tenure decisions coincide with fertility. Unless a woman is prepared to put off childbearing until her late thirties, it is difficult to combine career and children. The expectation that one will be found in the lab at 3 AM and at weekends conflicts with married and parental roles. Many women graduate students take a leave after pregnancy and do not return.

A major problem faced by women in research universities is that they have an absence of mentors and role models. Female faculty tend to be too few to form a critical mass that can work on behalf of female students. Many women Ph.D. prefer to go into industry or to teaching colleges, where the expectations are more compatible with marriage and child rearing, so this problem is self-perpetuating.

"You can have it all!" Rosalyn Yalow declared, but she didn't say it would be easy.

In the past 20 years, 3.5% of the Nobel Prizes in the sciences and economics have been awarded to women. But during the same period 24% of peace prizes and 25% of literature prizes have been won by women. Peace and literature laureates operate outside the formal, competitive institutions inhabited by scientists. Their achievements are nonetheless formidable and often require sacrifice. Aung San Suu Kyi, while under house arrest in Rangoon was not been able to see her two sons for years. She says she knows that "you have to make choices in life and give up some things. It's only the immature who think that they can have everything they want in life."

Toni Morrison (Literature 1993) writes:

> I don't go anywhere. I don't have any elaborate social life. I don't go anywhere to be happy, I don't go on vacations, I don't ski. I don't do any of the so-called fun things in life. Writing is what I do for me, that is where it is—where the vacation is, the fun is, the danger, the excitement—all of that is in my work.

The biographies and autobiographies of women laureates illuminate the bare statistics: the path to the Nobel Prize is more difficult for women than for men, and the personal costs are higher.

Chapter 8
An Outstanding Teacher
at a Critical Stage

A large number of Nobel laureates give credit for their success to a mentor who was influential in their intellectual development. We have already seen how Louis Germain, an elementary school teacher, was instrumental in launching Albert Camus' scholastic career. Barack Obama (Peace 2009) declared that "Every single one of us can point to a teacher who made a difference at some point in our lives." Glenn Seaborg (1951, Chemistry) quotes with approval the remark of Luis Alvarez (Physics, 1968) that "every scientist can recall the teacher who aroused his interest in a field." Among recent laureates, Tomas Lindahl (Chemistry, 2015), and Arthur McDonald (Physics, 2015) are two of many to pay public tribute to the influence of their teachers.

It was the opinion of André Lwoff (Medicine, 1965) that "The art of research is first of all to find a good *patron*." *Patron* in French means boss, but in this context it also carries the meaning of supervisor. The evidence on Nobel laureates appears to bear this out, showing how Nobel laureates teach and mentor younger scholars who become laureates in turn. Enrico Fermi (Physics, 1938), numbered five laureates among his students. Giuseppe Levi, professor of Anatomy at the University of Turin, and not himself a Nobel laureate, mentored three future laureates: Salvador Luria (Medicine 1969), Renato Dulbecco (Medicine 1975), and Rita Levi-Montalcini (Medicine 1986). The latter wrote:

> All three of us were students of the famous Italian histologist, Giuseppe Levi. We are indebted to him for a superb training in biological science, and for having learned to approach scientific problems in a most rigorous way at a time when such an approach was still unusual.

The Cavendish Laboratory at Cambridge was a factory for Nobel laureates. Under its first director, J. J. Thomson, it produced six Nobel laureates, and under Ernest Rutherford twelve. Eight alumni of Carl and Gerty Cori's lab at Washington University won Nobel Prizes. The Laboratory of Molecular Biology at Cambridge has produced fourteen Nobel Prizes, including Fred Sanger, who won the prize twice, as well as several prizes by scientists who have visited or done work at the Laboratory.

Zuckerman reports that:

> It is striking that more than half (48) of the 92 laureates who did their prize-winning research in the United States by 1972 had worked either as students, post doctorates, or junior collaborators under older Nobel laureates.

These 48 worked under 71 laureates. Paul Samuelson (Economics, 1970), in his Nobel acceptance speech, said, "I can tell you how to get a Nobel Prize. One condition is to have great teachers."

Hans Krebs made a similar point:

> If I ask myself how it came about that one day I found myself in Stockholm, I have not the slightest doubt that I owe this good fortune to the circumstance that I had an outstanding teacher at a critical stage in my scientific career when from my twenty-fifth to my twenty-ninth year I was associated with Otto Warburg in Berlin."

Otto Warburg (Medicine 1931) in turn had this to say:

> The most important event in the career of a young scientist is the personal contact with the great scientists of his time. Such an event happened to me in my life when Emil Fischer accepted me in 1903 as a co-worker.

On another occasion, when an American Ph.D. student sought his advice, Warburg wrote, "If you wish to become a scientist, you must ask a successful scientist to accept you in his laboratory, even if at the beginning you would only clean his test -tubes."

Finding an outstanding mentor is not simply a matter of luck. Zuckerman states that Nobel laureates "In their comparative youth, sometimes went to great lengths to make sure they would be working with those they considered the best in their field."

James Watson (Medicine, 1962) was an example, as described by François Jacob:

> Jim Watson was an amazing character. Tall, gawky, scraggly, he had an inimitable style. Inimitable in his dress: shirttails flying, knees in the air, socks down around his ankles. Inimitable in his bewildered manner, his mannerisms: his eyes always bulging, his mouth always open, he uttered short, choppy sentences punctuated by "Ah! Ah!" inimitable also in his way of entering a room, cocking his head like a rooster looking for the finest hen, to locate the most important scientist present and charging over to his side.

David Hubel (Medicine, 1981) urged students to seek out scientists in their field.

> If you hear about a scientist who appeals to your interests, look him or her up. Don't be shy, get some direct contact with people, including teachers, who are doing experiments.

André Lwoff became the *patron* of François Jacob (Medicine 1965); years later, they shared the Nobel Prize. How this mentorship came about is a tribute to Jacob's persistence.

François Jacob was born into middle class circumstances; his grandfather was the first Jewish general in the French army. When the Germans invaded France, Jacob was in his second year of medical school, planning to become a surgeon. "I considered the surgeon's profession the finest, the most noble in the world," he said. He escaped to Britain and joined the Free French Forces under De Gaulle, and was posted to the Second Armored Division. He spent the next four years in England, Senegal, Chad, Tunisia, Algeria, and France. He worked as a combat medic, and saw action several times. Of the twenty officers with whom he enlisted, only three survived. In 1944, he took part in the invasion of France, and was severely wounded by a bomb from a German plane while he was tending a wounded comrade in the open. He spent a year in hospital. His ambition to become a surgeon was dashed by his injuries, and he decided to pursue scientific research. He went to see André Lwoff, head of a biological laboratory at the Pasteur Institute. Lwoff told him that there were no staff vacancies. Jacob returned several times over a winter and spring, with the same result. He decided to make a last attempt in June, and this time, Lwoff said, "Go off on vacation and come back the first of September."

This is how Jacob describes Lwoff's mentorship.

> From the moment I crossed the threshold and was admitted into the clan of his pupils and friends, he showed me an unfailingly affectionate benevolence. He never ceased to encourage me, to show and to praise my work, to speed up promotion. And when I had grown up, when I began to make a stir, he continued, without taking umbrage, to push me forward. A rare virtue in a world motivated by ambition, by the need to shine, to be recognized. He looked at me, I believe, rather like a son, while I looked at him rather like a father.

In a tribute to Rutherford after his death, James Chadwick (Physics, 1935) spoke in similar terms. "He treated his students, even the most junior, as brother workers in the same field—and when necessary spoke to them 'like a father'". Every Sunday, at 4.30 PM, the students were invited to the Rutherfords' home for tea. Mark Oliphant said, "He drove us mercilessly, but we loved him for it."

Some mentors are uncompromising. Charles Huggins (Medicine, 1966) urged his younger colleagues: "Do not go to meetings, write books, or go to the library to find what to work on. They are a waste of time." If he felt that a faculty member was spending too much time in his office, he would slip a message under his door, which said, "With blood on the hands I have a chance, seated at the desk I have no chance."

One of the most influential and best-loved mentors of physicists was the Dane Niels Bohr (Physics, 1922). Bohr, son of a professor of physiology, keen skier, biker, and Olympic soccer player, studied under Rutherford, and published his model of atomic structure in 1913, which introduced the theory of electrons orbiting the nucleus of the atom. He won the Nobel Prize for physics in 1922 "for his services in the investigation of the structure of atoms and of the radiation emanating from them." From the 1920s to the 1950s, there were few leading physicists who did not spend some time in Bohr's laboratory in Copenhagen.

As the Nazis tightened their grip on the Jewish community in Germany, Bohr made his laboratory a place of refuge. He helped form the Danish Committee for the Support of Refugee Intellectuals, arranged for refugees to come to Denmark, and wrote to colleagues in other countries to secure employment for them. In 1941 he was visited by his former student, Werner Heisenberg (Physics, 1932). Their conversations went unrecorded, but it seems probable that Heisenberg wanted to discuss the development of atomic weapons; in any event, it led to a rift between the two men. After the Germans invaded Denmark, Bohr was closely watched by the Gestapo. He was frequently urged by American colleagues to take a position in the United States, but stayed at his post until he was advised that his arrest was imminent. He escaped to Sweden by fishing boat, and thence by plane to Britain. While in Sweden he aided in the rescue of the Danish Jews, most of whom escaped to Sweden by boat just before they were due to be rounded up. From Britain, Bohr went on to the United States to work on the Manhattan Project. Aware of the post-war dangers of nuclear weapons, he met with Churchill to urge the international control of atomic energy, but without success. At the end of the war he resumed his work in Copenhagen, where he died in 1962.

Affection between mentors and students goes both ways. In his speech at the Nobel banquet in 2011, the Chemistry laureate, Robert Lefkowitz, said:

> I have trained more than 200 students and fellows in my lab over the past 40 years, and a number of mine and Brian's trainees have traveled to Stockholm to share this experience with us. They are in a very real sense a second family. Many of our trainees are major leaders in our field of science, a source of enormous pride for both of us.

Related to the influence of a mentor is the influence of peers. Hans Krebs makes the point that "Association with a leading teacher almost automatically brings about close association with outstanding contemporaries of the pupil because great teachers tend to attract good people." Sheldon Glashow said simply, "What you become in life depends partly on who you go to school with." James Watson stressed the importance of associating with superior students: "Don't be the best in your class. If you're the best in your class you're in the wrong class."

Most of the examples given this far have been from the sciences. How far does the principle of mentoring apply to laureates in Literature and Peace?

In writing his most famous work, *The Waste Land*, T. S. Eliot (Literature, 1948) relied heavily on advice from Ezra Pound, but Pound was more a colleague than a mentor. Samuel Beckett (Literature, 1969) worked for some years with James Joyce, and was influenced by him. But in general, the solitary nature of writing and of learning to write means that mentorship is the exception, not the rule. Numerous universities today operate creative writing programs, but these do not appear to this point to have produced any Nobel Prize winners. (It could be argued that Eugene O'Neill (Literature, 1936) was an exception. He attended George Pierce Baker's celebrated course on playwriting at Harvard in 1914-1915.)

The situation is similar with respect to the Peace awards. Ralph Bunche (Peace, 1950) worked with Dag Hammarskjöld (Peace, 1961) at the United Nations, and said "Dag Hammarskjöld was the most remarkable man I have ever seen or worked with... I learned more from him than from any other man." Kofi Annan (Peace, 2001) is also an admirer of Hammarskjöld: "There can be no better rule of thumb for a Secretary-General, as he approaches each new challenge or crisis, than to ask himself, 'how would Hammarskjöld have handled this?'"

Martin Luther King (Peace, 1964) was deeply influenced by Mahatma Gandhi, who in turn was influenced by Tolstoy. King immersed himself in Gandhi's writings, visited India to learn more about him, and applied his doctrines of non-violence in his own work for civil rights. But in general, the peace laureates appear to develop their philosophies and their activities independently of the help of particular mentors.

Chapter 9
A Passion for Teaching

Nobel laureates, like many successful people, seize the opportunity to pass on their ideas to their students and to the public. One possible reason why they are so valued as mentors is that they are committed to the role of teacher.

Roald Hoffmann (Chemistry, 1981) said:

> I think research and teaching are absolutely inseparable. I hadn't really understood the empirical beauty of thermodynamics until I had to explain it to first-year students.

Teaching is viewed as hard work. Allvar Gullstrand (Medicine, 1911) said: "A professor whose hands do not shake by the end of the academic year has not performed his duties properly."

Similarly, Leon Lederman commented: "If you don't learn when you're teaching, then you're not doing it right." Glen Seaborg, who, as Chair of the Atomic Energy Commission, worked closely with several Presidents, observed that:

> To teach, you really have to know your material, and I took preparation for the classroom as seriously as getting ready for a meeting with the President of the United States.

Robert Solow (Economics, 1987) said, "If you're worth your pay you ask yourself before every class, what is the best way to get this stuff across to these kids?"

While teaching at a university in Brazil in 1952, Richard Feynman wrote himself a note that would have pleased many educational theorists: "First figure out why you want the students to learn the subject and what you want them to know, and the method will result more or less by common sense."

Peter Kapitsa (Physics 1978) also recognized the importance of teaching: "Having students and working with the young generation is the best way in which a scientist can retain the vigor of youth and keep pace with the advances of science." He also said, "The history of science tells us that an outstanding scientist is not necessarily a great man, but a great teacher must be a great man."

After winning the Nobel Prize, Carl Wieman (Physics, 2001) devoted increasing time to the issue of science teaching. He said, "Although I don't have a passion for teaching, I do have a passion. I have a passion for students learning."

Richard Feynman shared this passion:

> I find that teaching and the students keep life going, and I would *never* accept any position in which somebody has invented a happy situation for me where I don't have to teach. Never.

Gabriela Mistral (Literature, 1945), who worked for many years as a teacher, said, "To teach and to love intensely means to arrive at the last day with the spear of Longinus piercing the heart aflame with love." J. J. Thomson (Physics, 1906) recognized the interplay of teaching and research: "There is no better way of getting a good grasp of your subject, or one more likely to start more ideas for research, than teaching it." Daniel Tsui (Physics, 1998) said, "Perhaps it was the Confucius in me, the faint voice I often heard when I was alone, that the only meaningful life is a life of learning. What better way is there to learn than through teaching?"

Nobel laureates in literature often hold professorial appointments. One of them, Czeslaw Milosz (Literature, 1980) spoke of the satisfaction that teaching produces:

> Only my pedagogic career, begun late in life, around age fifty, has afforded me some lasting satisfaction. In the lecture hall, facing the young people to whom I was able to offer something, I forgot about my wretchedness and felt that I had a right to exist.

John Steinbeck thought highly of teaching: "I have come to believe that a great teacher is a great artist and that there are as few as there are any other great artists." Richard Taylor (Physics, 1990) thought equally highly of teachers: "One thing that hasn't changed since I went to school is the genuine commitment teachers have to the success of their students."

In 1987, When Toni Morrison was named the Robert F. Goheen Professor in the Council of Humanities at Princeton University, she said, "I take teaching as seriously as I do my writing."

Whether or not Nobel laureates regard themselves as professional teachers, once they receive the prize, they are in instant and constant demand as speakers, lecturers, and writers. Desmond Tutu (Peace, 1984) and the Dalai Lama (Peace, 1989) immediately come to mind. Most seem to adapt readily to this role. Being passionate about their work, they are happy to share their passion with others.

Chapter 10
Our Friendship Unfolded
Like an Epic Poem

"The popular mind imagines the scientist as a lonely genius," wrote Michael Bishop (Medicine, 1989). "In reality, few of us are geniuses, and even fewer are lonely."

Sydney Brenner (Medicine , 2002) agreed:

> The whole idea that science is conducted by people working alone in rooms and struggling with the forces of nature is absolutely ridiculous. It is a social activity of the highest sort.

In this respect, a trend toward collaboration is apparent in the history of Nobel Prizes. In the first year the prizes were awarded, 1901, the peace prize was divided between Henri Dunant and Frédéric Passy. All the other prizes were undivided. Wilhelm Röntgen, who won the prize for physics, was a typical lone researcher of the era. Röntgen, born in 1845, was even as a child good with his hands and interested in nature. He took his Ph.D. at the University of Zurich, and after teaching at a number of universities, ended up as Professor of Physics at the University of Munich. He was working on cathode rays one evening in 1895 when he discovered that objects placed in their path showed variable transparency when recorded on a photographic plate. As the nature of the new rays was unknown, he called them x-rays. One of the first x-ray photographs he took was of his wife's hand. It clearly showed the bones and the ring she was wearing, and more faintly the flesh of the hand which was more permeable to the rays.

Like Röntgen, most of the early science laureates worked alone. In the first 10 years that the prizes were offered (1901-1910), only 5 of the 30 science prizes were shared. By contrast, in the last 10 years, (2005-2014), 27 of the 31 science prizes were shared. Science has become a much more collaborative enterprise, and the problem for the Nobel committees has become one of identifying a maximum of three scientists to be honored from research teams that are often large.

While Röntgen was typical of the isolated scientist of his era, the early years of the prize provide at least one example of collaboration, that of Pierre and Marie Curie, who shared the prize for physics with Henri Becquerel in 1903.

Madame Curie, née Maria Sklodowska, was born in Warsaw in 1867, the daughter of a secondary school teacher. She was educated in local schools and became involved in student revolutionary politics. In 1891 she moved to Paris to continue her education at the Sorbonne, where she obtained Licenciateships in Physics and Mathematics. She lived in a fifth-floor walk-up apartment, and had to study night and day to catch up with her peers who had graduated from French Lycées. In 1895 she married Pierre Curie, a physicist at the Sorbonne. The marriage was marked by close scientific collaboration and profound emotional attachment. In 1896 Henri Becquerel (Physics, 1903) had discovered radioactivity, and the Curies undertook to isolate the radioactive element, radium. The School of Physics at the Sorbonne provided an old unheated shed with a leaking roof and a dirt floor, where the Curies worked for years, freezing in winter and sweltering in summer:

> And yet it was in this miserable old shed that the best and happiest years of our life were spent, entirely consecrated to work. I sometimes passed the whole day stirring a mass in ebullition, with an iron rod nearly as big as myself. In the evening I was broken with fatigue.

Despite his eminent qualifications, Pierre Curie was repeatedly passed over for a professorial chair, and to make ends meet had to assume mundane teaching responsibilities. It was only after winning the Nobel Prize that he was elected to the Academy of Science and a chair of physics was created for him at the Sorbonne. A laboratory was not provided during his lifetime.

Their researches were rewarded by success, and the Curies received the Nobel Prize for Physics in 1903. The prize money was welcome, but the Curies refused to patent radium, or to sell the radium they had refined, both of which would have brought them great wealth.

Tragedy quickly followed when Pierre Curie was run over and killed by a heavy goods wagon on a Paris street in 1906. In her private diary,

Marie wrote, "Everything is over, Pierre is sleeping his last sleep beneath the earth; it is the end of everything, everything, everything." The university broke with precedent by appointing Marie to Pierre's professorship, the first woman in France to be so honored. There she taught the only course in the world on radioactivity.

An emotionally turbulent period occurred a few years later when the press publicized and condemned Marie's affair with a married scientist, Paul Langevin. Marie nevertheless continued with her scientific research, which included studying the therapeutic uses of radioactivity. When she was finally given a laboratory, she donated to it the gram of radium she and Pierre had isolated, worth a million francs. Her work was recognized by a second Nobel Prize, for chemistry, in 1911. Her daughter Irene Joliot-Curie also became a physicist, and with her husband won the Nobel Prize for Physics in 1935. Marie Curie died in 1934, from leukemia almost certainly caused by long-term exposure to radioactive materials. The same disease killed her daughter Irene in 1956.

Always modest and unassuming, never impressed by wealth or fame, Marie Curie summarized her philosophy in the words, "Work gives life the sweet taste of happiness"

François Jacob and Jacques Monod, of the Pasteur Institute in Paris, won the Nobel Prize for Medicine in 1965, together with the head of their laboratory, André Lwoff. In his remarkable memoir, *The Statue Within* , Jacob describes their collaboration:

> Between us we wove an intellectual relationship of exceptional intensity, open intimacy. Each day we spent several hours together, morning and evening, computing the results of experiments, analyzing them, criticizing them, drawing inferences, rectifying hypotheses, concocting new experiments. Singing a cantata, whistling a quartet. Also joking. For all this went on in an atmosphere both feverish and gay where each teased the other at every turn... Very quickly we had reached a rare degree of complicity, our discussions moved at top speed, in bursts of brief retorts, like a ping-pong match. Scarcely had one begun a sentence than the other answered without waiting for the end... The harmony between us was so close, our repartee so quick, our train of ideas so coordinated, that it was often difficult to say which was the first to come up with a hypothesis or propose an experiment... For close to five years, our friendship unfolded like an epic poem.

Francis Crick, who together with James Watson and Maurice Wilkins won the prize for Medicine in 1962 for their discovery of the structure of DNA, pointed to one of the criteria for successful collaboration:

> You must be perfectly candid, one might almost say rude, to the person you are working with. It is useless working with someone who is either much too junior than yourself, or much too senior, because then politeness creeps in, and this is the end of all good collaboration in science.

A fine example of collaboration is provided by Daniel Kahneman, who won the prize for economics in 2002, and who collaborated for several years with Amos Tversky.

> We were not just having fun. I quickly discovered that Amos had a remedy for everything I found difficult about writing. No wet-mush problem for him: he had an uncanny sense of direction. With him, movement was always forward. Progress might be slow, but each of the myriad of successive drafts that we produced was an improvement—this was not something I could take for granted when working on my own. Amos's work was always characterized by confidence and by a crisp elegance, and it was a joy to find those characteristics now attached to my ideas as well. As we were writing our first paper, I was conscious of how much better it was than the more hesitant piece I would have written by myself. I don't know exactly what it was that Amos found to like in our collaboration—we were not in the habit of trading compliments—but clearly he was also having a good time. We were a team, and we remained in that mode for well over a decade. The Nobel Prize was awarded for work that we produced during that period of intense collaboration.

Amos Tversky died in 1996, six years before Daniel Kahneman was awarded the Nobel Prize.

Two married collaborators were Carl and Gerty Cori, who shared the prize for Medicine in 1947. Both were born in Prague, and they met when they were studying at the Medical School of the German University of Prague, from which they graduated in 1920. When they married, Gerti converted from Judaism to Roman Catholicism. Their scientific collaboration began when they were medical students, and endured throughout their careers. In addition to their common research interests, they shared a passion for hiking, skiing, swimming, tennis, and mountain climbing. Foreseeing political turmoil in Europe, they moved to the United States in 1922, to work at the State Institute for the Study of Malignant Diseases in Buffalo, New York. There they published 50 papers together. It was in Buffalo that they did the work on the Cori cycle, the movement of energy from muscles to liver and back to muscle, that later won them the Nobel Prize. They moved to the School of Medicine at Washington University, St. Louis, in 1931, where Carl became head of the pharmacology department; Gerty was offered only a research assistantship at one-tenth of her husband's salary, but later was made professor. They were awarded the Nobel Prize "for their discovery of the course of the catalytic conversion of glycogen." In his acceptance speech, Carl Cori said:

> Our collaboration began thirty years ago when we were still medical students at the University of Prague and has continued ever since. Our efforts have been largely complementary, and one without the other would not have gone as far as in combination.

Gerty Cori suffered from myelofibrosis for the last ten years of her life, dying in 1957. She summed up her attitude to her work in this way:

> The love for and dedication to one's work seems to me to be the basis for happiness. For a research worker, the unforgotten moments of his life are those rare ones, which come after years of plodding work, when the veil over nature's secret seems suddenly to lift and when what was dark and chaotic suddenly appears in a clear and beautiful light and pattern.

Even in the case of scientists whose work was essentially solitary, there is an awareness of their dependence on the work of others. Einstein observed that:

> A hundred times every day I remind myself that my inner and outer life depend on the labors of other men, living and dead, and

that I must exert myself in order to give in the same measure as I have received.

While collaboration is the norm in the sciences, it is virtually unknown in the arts. There have been no Nobel Prizes awarded for collaborative literary endeavour. While musicals and movies are the work of many hands, literary works, with rare exceptions, are the work of a single individual. As Ernest Hemingway put it in his Nobel acceptance speech, "Writing, at its best, is a lonely life... He does his work alone and if he is a good enough writer he must face eternity, or the lack of it, each day."

The Peace prize is also normally offered to individuals who have often pursued a lonely course in their promotion of peace or justice. An exception was the award in 1976 to two Irish peace activists, Mairead Corrigan and Betty Williams.

The path that led Betty Williams and Mairead Corrigan to the Nobel Peace Prize began with a tragedy. In 1976, British soldiers shot a suspected IRA driver; his vehicle went out of control, killing three children, who were nieces and nephews of Mairead Corrigan. This event was witnessed by Betty Williams. The mother of the three children, Anne Maguire, committed suicide in 1980. With the aunt of the children, Mairead Corrigan, Betty Williams organized a peace petition, obtaining 6000 names. They founded Women for Peace, which became The Community for Peace People. They led peace marches to the graves of the children, attracting up to 35,000 people. Numerous other marches followed, in Northern Ireland and in other parts of Britain. Peace Committees were established in many towns and cities. Assistance was given to paramilitaries who wanted to escape from their organization. "All I want to do," said Betty Williams, "is to take a bomb out of a kid's hand and put a tennis racket in it."

The path of peace was itself not always peaceful. The peace marchers were frequently stoned and attacked. On one occasion, Betty Williams invited two women supporters of the Provisional IRA into her home, where they beat her brutally.

In 1976, the Nobel Peace Prize was awarded to Betty Williams and Mairead Corrigan, in recognition that "their initiative paved the way for the strong resistance against violence and misuse of power which was present in broad circles of the people."

After the award of the Nobel Prize, Betty Williams and her husband divorced; she remarried and moved to the United States, where she lectured extensively, returning to Northern Ireland in 2004. She has been awarded The People's Peace Prize of Norway, the Schweitzer Medallion for Courage, the Martin Luther King Award, and the Eleanor Roosevelt Award.

At 32, Mairead Corrigan was the youngest person to win the Peace Prize. At the time, she was working as a secretary, and as a volunteer with a Catholic lay organization. She married Jackie MacGuire, the widower of her sister Anne. In 1990 she was awarded the Pacem in Terris Award, and has received many other honors and awards. In 2006, she was one of the founders of the Nobel Women's Initiative, established to support work towards women's rights.

In general, we may say that ability to collaborate is today essential for scientific achievement; but achievement in literature and peace requires the ability to work alone.

Chapter 11
You Might Have Thought
I Was a Strange Kid

Incipient genius shows up in various ways in the early lives of Nobel laureates. When the economist George Akerlof (Economics, 2001) was asked in second grade what he wanted for Christmas, he said "A steel mill". Asked by his father, Arthur Kornberg (Chemistry, 1959), the same question as a child, Roger Kornberg (Chemistry, 2006) said, "A week in the lab". At age 7, Joshua Lederberg (Medicine, 1958) wrote, "I would like to be a scientist of mathematics like Einstein. I would study Science and discover a few theories in science."

Gerardus 't Hooft (Physics, 1999) tells the following anecdote:

> One day, a school teacher asked all the kids in my class, "What do you want to do in your life?" I was trying to say that I wanted to be a professor, but at that moment I couldn't think of the word. Instead I said I wanted to be "a man who knew everything."

Linda Buck, who shared the prize for medicine in 2004, said, "You might have thought I was a strange kid for the things I did. I buried my hamster after it died, then dug it up a while later to see what it looked like." Konrad Lorenz discovered imprinting as a child, when he was given a day-old duckling by a neighbor. Many of the scientists had chemistry sets and in some cases home laboratories when quite young, as Horst Stormer (Physics, 1998) reports:

> I built a rocket that propelled a modified car of a toy train into the air. After several exhilarating launches, the rocket exploded in my hand and ripped off half my right thumb. I learned an important lesson: a rocket and a bomb differ only in the exhaust.

Douglas Osheroff (Physics, 1996) remarked:

I think I was genetically predisposed to become a scientist. As a child, I got into all kinds of things, many of which would get me into trouble with the FBI today.

Many Nobel laureates were early and voracious readers; public libraries played an important part in many of their lives. They attended a wide variety of elementary and secondary schools. The current record is held by the Bronx High School of Science, which has graduated eight future laureates. Marlborough College, a private secondary school in Britain, has produced three.

Laureates tend to go through their formal education at speed. John Bardeen (Physics, 1956 and 1972) skipped from third to seventh grade. Sydney Brenner went to the University of Witwatersrand at 14, and qualified as a doctor at 20. James Watson and John Bardeen, who won the Nobel Prize in chemistry twice (1956 and 1972) both graduated from high school at 15. Several Nobels, including Enrico Fermi and Max Planck received their Ph.Ds. at the age of 21. William Ramsey (Chemistry, 1904) earned his at 20. So did Robert Woodward (Chemistry, 1965), despite being suspended by MIT for a semester for "inattention to formal studies". Harriet Zuckerman found that American science Nobels received the doctorate at a mean age of 24.8, compared with a median age of 26 for all doctorates.

The youngest person to receive a Nobel Prize was Malala Yousafzai of Pakistan, who won the Peace Prize in 1914 at 17. Harriet Zuckerman found that American Nobel laureates in science won the prize at a mean age of 48.6 years; they did their prize-winning work eleven years earlier, at 37.6 years. Later statistics, for 20th century Nobel laureates, compiled by Baruch Shalev, are shown in Table 5.

Table 5
Age of Nobel laureates at time of publication of prize-winning work and interval to receiving prize

Category	Publication Age	Interval to Prize
Physics	37.3	15.4
Chemistry	40.7	15.0
Medicine	41.1	15.2
Peace	54.3	9.1

| Literature | 57.4 | 6.3 |
| Economics | 59.0 | 8.3 |

Two Russian researchers, V. N. Anisimov and A. I. Mikhal'skii, found that the gap between discovery and prize in chemistry widened during the twentieth century, from 13 years in 1901-1925 to 24 years in 1975-2003. There was a corresponding increase in the age at which the award was made. From the first to the last quarter of the century, the number of chemistry laureates over 61 went from 23% to 53%, and the number under 40 decreased from 19% to 3%.

The delays in recognition are sometimes lengthy. Einstein did his groundbreaking work on relativity in 1905 when he was 26; he had to wait until he was 43 for the prize, which was then awarded for his work on the photoelectric effect. Karl Landsteiner developed the classification of blood groups in 1901, but had to wait until 1930 for his Nobel Prize. Chandrasekhar had to wait half a century for his work on black holes to be recognized by the Nobel committee. Similarly, Ernst Ruska was awarded the Nobel Prize in physics in 1986 when he was 80, for the electron microscope, which he invented in 1933 at the age of 27. On the other hand, Banting and Macleod were awarded the prize in 1923 for the discovery of insulin the previous year.

James Watson exaggerated slightly when he claimed that "Almost every important new discovery comes from someone under thirty-five." Sheldon Glashow (Physics, 1979) said, "Most of the progress in understanding how the universe works is made by people under 40, which is just as well, or we'd end up like the Kremlin run by people over 80."

Paul Dirac (Physics, 1933) wrote that:

> Age is, of course, a fever chill
> That every physicist must fear
> He's better dead than living still
> Once he's past his thirtieth year.

Leo Esaki (Physics, 1973) recognized that a certain period of life is critical:

The most precious, creative and innovative period in your life is the 10-year period around the age of 32. Plan your career path to use this precious 10-year period wisely and effectively to produce your greatest achievement in your life.

The evidence suggests that Nobel laureates achieve their breakthrough work about 20 years after they begin their undergraduate studies. Malcolm Gladwell argues that it takes approximately 10,000 hours of training and practice to accomplish a major achievement. If we calculate from the beginning of doctoral studies, and assume that Nobel laureates work a 2500 hour year, the total would be 37,500 hours.

James Watson is a classic example of a whiz-kid. Born in 1928, son of a businessman, he entered the University of Chicago at 15. He graduated with a degree in zoology. A long-abiding interest in ornithology gave way to a passion for genetics. He applied for graduate work at Harvard but was turned down, and went to Indiana University, where he had the good fortune to work with the Nobel geneticist H. J. Muller (Medicine, 1946). His thesis was supervised by another Nobel laureate, Salvador Luria, a microbiologist. Luria arranged for him to do post-doctoral work at the Cavendish Laboratory in Cambridge. He had already met and shared ideas with Maurice Wilkins (Medicine, 1962). In Cambridge, he met Francis Crick, and together they solved the mystery of the structure of DNA.

Watson was specific about the ingredients of success. One of his later books is entitled *Avoid Boring People*. In that book, he says, "Never be the brightest person in a room." In 1993 he summarized his rules for success:

> To succeed in science, you need a lot more than luck… The first rule: To succeed in science, you have to avoid dumb people… My second rule: to make a huge success, a scientist has to be prepared to get into deep trouble. My third rule: Be sure you always have someone up your sleeve, who will save you when you find yourself in deep shit… My fourth rule: Never do anything that bores you… My final rule is: If you can't stand to be with your real peers, get out of science.

While Watson's career barely meets the 10,000 hour rule—he was only 25 when he co-discovered the double helix—he conforms with the pattern that Nobel laureates frequently seek out and are mentored by other Nobel laureates.

Another exception to the 10,000 hour rule was William Lawrence Bragg, who shared the Nobel Prize in physics with his father, William Henry Bragg, in 1915. He was the youngest person up to the present to win a Nobel Prize in science. He was born in Adelaide, Australia, where his father was Head of Physics at the university. He took first class honors in mathematics at the University of Adelaide in 1908. The next year the family moved to Leeds, in northern England, and Lawrence Bragg entered Trinity College, Cambridge, where he obtained a degree in physics with first class honors in 1912. He collaborated with his father on X-ray analysis of crystal structure, for which they were jointly awarded the Nobel Prize in 1915. He spent the years 1915-1919 in the army, where he worked on sound ranging methods of locating enemy artillery, earning the Order of the British Empire and the Military Cross. He subsequently became a professor at Manchester University and eventually head of the Cavendish Laboratory at Cambridge.

The Braggs represented a successful case of cross-age collaboration. As scientists age, they find it necessary to associate with the young, both for the intellectual stimulation and to keep abreast of advances of science. Albert Szent-Gyorgyi (Medicine, 1937) affirmed this:

> When one gets older, one is more sensitive—one likes youth because one needs youth. It is a wrong idea to have old people around when you are old. You need youth to keep you young and active.

John B. Fenn (Chemistry, 2002) felt the same at the age of 85:

> I go to the lab every day. Whether I accomplish much in the way of research, I don't know. But we are working on problems, and I try to encourage students to look at this or look at that or look at the other thing, and I get a lot of nourishment from their young red blood cells. I'm a vampire, essentially.

Selman Waksman (Medicine, 1952) paid a similar tribute: "I can truthfully say that I owe much to my professors, that I owe more to my colleagues, but that I owe most to my students."

James Watson states a paradox:

> The chief rule above 65 is to avoid old people. But, see, when you're young, you should also avoid young people because you won't learn from them.

A strain of nostalgia runs through the words of Nobel laureates for a youth in which it appears scientific research and collaboration were more carefree. Here is Watson again:

> I often have the sense that I still belong to that half-mad, but uniquely wonderful, playing field of my youth, where the aim was the truth, not money, and where decency always took precedence over cunning.

Peter Kapitsa (Physics, 1978) referred nostalgically to his early years when he worked with Rutherford:

> The year that Rutherford died there disappeared forever the happy days of free scientific work which gave us such delight in our youth. Science has lost her freedom. Science has become a productive force. She has become rich but she has become enslaved and part of her is veiled in secrecy. I do not know whether Rutherford would continue nowadays to joke and laugh as he used to do.

For the scientist, the "golden years" are the years spent in the laboratory, before seniority or fame remove him or her for service on committees or commissions, or in administrative capacities. In the overwhelming number of cases, it is in their twenties that scientists serve the apprenticeship that ultimately leads to discovery. There is no evidence that the hard work and fast pace of laureates' early years shortens their lives. Two laureates to date have lived to a hundred—Rita Levi-Montalcini (Medicine, 1986) died at 103 in 2012, and Ronald Coase (Economics, 1991) died in 2013 at 102. The oldest person to receive a Nobel Prize was Leonid Hurwicz, who won the prize for economics in 2007, at the age of 90.

Matthew Rablen and Andrew Oswald examined the laureates in Physics and Chemistry for 1901-1950, and found that they lived to an average of 77.18 years. When they compared laureates with scientists who were nominated but did not receive the Nobel Prize, they found that laureates lived 1.62 years longer. They reference Fathersdata showing that occupational status is related to longevity.

Table 6 shows the age at award, expected age at death, and actual age at death for laureates in the different categories. Expected age at death is based on life expectancy at the time when they won the Prize. The data used is based on figures for males in the United Kingdom in 1980, provided by the UK Office for National Statistics.

Table 6

Category	age at prize	expected age	actual age at death
Chemistry	52.4	74.6	80.0
Economics	66.5	82.0	83.1
Literature	63.8	80.6	79.0
Medicine	56.3	76.9	78.0
Peace	62.0	79.6	77.4
Physics	52.4	74.6	80.0

The 'age reward' associated with being a Nobel laureate appears to apply in the sciences, but not to literature or peace laureates. The average age at death for Nobel peace prize laureates includes the four laureates (Anwar Sadat, Martin Luther King, Yitzak Rabin, and Carl von Ossietzky) who died prematurely by assassination, or, in the case of Ossietzky, abuse.

Charles Townes, who won the Nobel Prize for Physics in 1964, was asked what was the secret of a long life—he was then 89 years old—he replied:

> Some people say I work hard: I come in on Saturdays, and I work evenings both at my desk and in the lab. But I think I'm just having a good time doing physics and science.

Like Townes, most Nobel laureates scorn retirement. Rita Levi-Montalcini said, "The moment you stop working, you are dead... For me, it would be unhappiness beyond anything else." Ernest Hemingway declared that:

> Retirement is the filthiest word in the language. Whether by choice or by fate, to retire from what you do—and what you do makes you what you are—is to back up into the grave.

Writers, scientists, and peace activists tend to work until they drop. On his deathbed, Jacques Monod's last words were "I am seeking to understand."

An exception was George Sanger. He won the prize for Chemistry in 1958 and again in 1980. On the eve of his 65th birthday he worked in the lab until the end of the day, then closed the door and never entered it again, devoting himself to growing roses and sailing his yacht.

Chapter 12
Get Married Young
and Stay Married

Marital stability may be a factor in the success of Nobel laureates. Certainly they have a lower divorce rate than the general population. The proportion of marriages that end in divorce is estimated at about 44% in the United States and 38% in Canada. For American billionaires, the rate is 30%. The divorce rate for Nobel laureates in the 20th century was approximately 10.6%. The figures for the different categories of laureate are Physics 5.9%, Peace 6.0%, Chemistry 7.8%, Medicine 8.2%, Economics 13.3%, and Literature 33.3%.

We must take into account that these figures include marriages from early in the 20th century when, and in societies where, the divorce rate is lower than currently in the United States. Nevertheless, the degree of difference between Nobel laureates and the general population seems apparent. What accounts for this?

One Nobel laureate who addressed this issue was the double prize winner, Linus Pauling (Chemistry, 1954; Peace,1962). His advice to young scientists was:

> You should look around carefully at the members of the opposite sex, and pick one out that you'd like to be with all your life. Get married young, and stay married.

It seems likely that Nobel laureates make good choices of lifetime companions, just as they make good choices in their lifetime work. Marriage provides a support system, and it is best for a career if this support system is stable and is not disrupted.

The averages mask the outliers. Bertrand Russell (Literature, 1950) and Ernest Hemingway were both married four times. Saul Bellow (Literature, 1976) was married five times. The data also includes people who were never married, such as Mother Teresa (Peace, 1979), the Dalai Lama (Peace, 1989), and Father Georges Pire (Peace, 1958).

Not all Nobel laureates lead conventional private lives. Erwin Schrödinger was an Austrian non-Jewish scientist who detested the Nazis. His mother was half English, and he learned English as a child. He met the British scientist Professor Frederick Lindemann in Berlin, where Schrödinger was head of physics at the Kaiser Wilhelm Institute. Lindemann was recruiting German scientists, and Schrödinger expressed interest in going to England. Lindemann arranged for funding and for a fellowship at Oxford. Schrödinger asked Lindemann if he could also arrange for an appointment for his assistant, Arthur March, also non-Jewish. According to Jean Medawar and David Pyke, the reason was that Schrödinger was in love with March's wife. By the time they arrived in England she was pregnant by him. Schrödinger arrived in Oxford the same day that his Nobel Prize was announced. But he did not find Oxford to his taste, and returned briefly to Austria. There he wrote a fawning letter to Hitler; when news of the letter appeared in Nature, Schrödinger's reputation in England suffered severely. Meanwhile, the Irish Prime Minister, Aemon de Valera, had established an Institute for Advanced Study in Dublin, and invited Schrödinger to head the School of Theoretical Physics. Schrödinger accepted the invitation and stayed there for sixteen years. He lived in a middle-class Dublin suburb with his wife and his mistress, while simultaneously carrying on affairs with a number of his students, and fathering children with two Irish women. In 1956 he retired and returned to Vienna.

Divorce and the Nobel Prize are sometimes directly connected. Einstein was confident enough of eventually winning the prize that he made the award money part of his divorce settlement in 1919. He won the prize in 1921, when it was worth 121,572 Swedish kroner, i.e. $32,250. Similarly, a clause in the divorce settlement of the economist Robert Lucas (Economics, 1995) read, "Wife shall receive 50 percent of any Nobel Prize" if won within 7 years of divorce on 31 October 1988; he won 10 October 1995, so had to split the $600,000. He remarked: "A deal is a deal. It's hard to be unpleasant after winning a prize like that."

Chapter 13
Go Out on a Limb

"Go out on a limb," said Jimmy Carter (Peace, 2002), "that's where the fruit is." The willingness to go beyond conventional truth is a major factor in the success of Nobel laureates. The essence of discovery is the replacement of ignorance or error by a new truth. This frequently puts future Nobel laureates at odds with their peers and their nominal superiors.

Barry Marshall (Medicine 2005) may be taken to represent scientists who struggle to have their findings accepted by the scientific community. He made a hugely important medical discovery, but experienced years of rejection and ridicule before it was universally acknowledged.

Marshall was born in 1951 in Western Australia. His father was a mechanical fitter and turner, and his mother was training as a nurse. The family moved a good deal, eventually settling in Perth for its educational opportunities. Marshall grew up in an atmosphere of experimentation and exploration,- making slingshots, crystal sets, electromagnets, and "in the tradition of Alfred Nobel, we would create various explosive mixtures and make firecrackers and bombs." He did well in school and after considering electrical engineering, chose to enter medical school, graduating in 1975. A rotation in gastroenterology in 1981 first stimulated his interest in stomach ulcers. Together with Robin Warren (Medicine, 2005), he studied cases and the literature and observed the presence of characteristically curved bacteria in stomach ulcers, eventually named helicobacter pylori. Meanwhile, his hobby of electronics enabled him to build and use computers for research and communication and to "function better as a single unfunded scientist than many units with multiple support staff." His medical training complete, he took a position as senior registrar at Fremantle Hospital where he was able to continue his research.

The prevailing medical dogma was that the cause of stomach ulcers was excess stomach acid due to stress and poor diet. Warren and Marshall's conclusion, based on clinical studies, that bacteria were the cause was not readily accepted. Although a number of researchers in various countries began to replicate and confirm Marshall's findings, his work continued to be rejected or delayed for publication. *The Lancet* published letters by Marshall and Warren, but Marshall's paper, on helicobacter pylori in gastritis and duodenal and gastric ulcers, was rejected in 1983 by the Gastroenterological Society of Australia. He encountered constant criticism that his conclusions were premature and not well supported, that the bacteria were either contaminants or harmless. These views were so tenaciously held that Marshall asked, "Was gastroenterology a science or a religion? I decided it was the latter." Animal experiments were not entirely satisfactory, what was needed was experimental data on a human subject. It was at this point that Marshall conducted his famous self-experiment. Convinced that helicobacter pylori was the cause of stomach ulcers, he describes what he did next:

> We mixed up a complete flourishing growth of bacteria from a petri dish—we calculated out later that it was a thousand million bacteria—and mixed it up, and I said, "Well, here it goes, down the hatch." And my lab technician, who was fairly conventional, he was horrified. He was waiting for me to drop dead.

He quickly became ill, suffering painful gastritis, vomiting, appetite loss, and halitosis. Two endoscopies confirmed the infection and ulcerative damage to the stomach mucosa. He maintained the experiment for two weeks, until his wife insisted he terminate it. A course of antibiotics soon cured the condition.

Marshall was now successfully treating patients who had suffered peptic ulcers for years with a two week course of antibiotics and bismuth. Proctor and Gamble became interested, developing a bismuth drug and patenting much of Marshall's work. In 1986, Marshall moved to the University of Virginia where he spent the next ten years. The role of helicobacter in peptic ulcers was still not widely accepted in the United States. But the media became interested in his research, and gradually the tide of acceptance began to turn. In 1994, the National Institutes of Health held a consensus conference in Washington which ended with the statement that the key to gastric ulcers was detection and eradication of Helicobacter pylori.

The Marshalls moved back to Perth in 1996. In 2005, he and Robin Warren shared the Nobel Prize for Medicine "for their discovery of the bacterium *Helicobacter pylori* and its role in gastritis and peptic ulcer disease."

Paul Lauterbuhr, who won the Nobel Prize for Medicine in 2003, put the dilemma of the ground-breaking scientist this way: "There's a saying among scientists, that you don't know you've got a really good idea until at least three Nobel laureates have told you it's wrong."

Sydney Brenner would have agreed:

> I always believed that the best thing in science is to work out of phase. That is, either half a wavelength ahead or half a wavelength behind. It doesn't matter. As long as you're out of phase with the fashion you can do new things!

Such an approach is not without costs, as Corneille Heymans (Medicine, 1938) remarked:

> When you have made a new discovery, people begin by saying that it is not true; then when the truth of what you have proposed becomes absolutely evident, they say that it is not you who discovered it.

While many Nobel laureates have to struggle to get their ideas accepted, not many are terminated from their jobs in the process. That was the case with Werner Forssmann.

When Werner Forssmann was awarded the Nobel Prize for Medicine in 1956, many people asked, who is Werner Forssmann? The answer was, a urologist practicing in a small town in Germany. Forssmann himself said, "I feel like a village parson who has just learned that he has been made bishop."

Werner Forssmann was born in Berlin in 1904, where he attended the classical gymnasium and university. His father was killed in World War I. Influenced by his uncle--a country doctor, he qualified in medicine in 1929, and went to the University Medical Clinic for clinical training. For clinical instruction in surgery he went to the August Victoria Home in Eberswalde, near Berlin. It was here that he became dissatisfied with the inaccuracy and uncertainty of heart diagnosis, and developed a technique for catheterization of the heart beginning with experiments on animals. One evening, he anaesthetized his elbow, then inserted an aneurism needle under the vein, opened it and pushed a catheter in until an x-ray showed the tip of the catheter inside the heart, in the right ventricle. He took X-ray photos for evidence.

The importance of this experiment was that it paved the way for direct observation and measurement of cardiac activity. In time, cardiac catheterization became crucially important in assessment and treatment of shock, heart disease, and other conditions. But at the time, its importance was not appreciated. He published his findings in an article, "Probing the Right Ventricle of the Heart" in 1929. The response by his director was "Get out! Leave my department immediately!" Forssmann catheterized his own heart a total of nine times. But few other clinics followed his lead, and he was subjected to accusations of irresponsibility and of violating medical ethics, which prevented him from pursuing much further this line of enquiry. In his memoirs, he writes:

> For years I was amazed, disappointed and distressed by the lack of understanding, prejudice and bitter hostility that greeted my work. Only now in old age do I realize that I had engaged not only in a battle to develop cardiology, but also in psychological warfare to overcome primitive prejudice in modern man.

Cardiac catheterization only became accepted after its use by André Cournand and Dickinson Richards was approved by the Columbia University College of Physicians and Surgeons in New York during World War II. Cournand and Richards shared the Nobel Prize with Werner Forssmann in 1956.

Forssmann moved to various hospitals and undertook specialized training in urology. He was a chief of surgery at two hospitals and a reserve officer when World War II broke out. Throughout the war, Forssmann served as a medical officer, reaching the rank of Surgeon-Major, and serving on both eastern and western fronts. At one point, to his great distaste, he was assigned to supervise executions at Brandenburg-Görden Penitentiary. Here victims, notably conscientious objectors, were executed by guillotine; Forssmann's job was to witness the executions and certify that death had taken place. At war's end, cut off and surrounded by Russians, Forssmann escaped by swimming the Elbe under fire, to become a prisoner of the Americans.

On his release, he was barred from senior medical posts because he had joined the Nazi Party in the 1930s. He became a country doctor in the Black Forest, and then took up the practice of urology with his wife in Bad Kreusnach.

Forssmann summarized his philosophy of medicine in his Nobel lecture: "One may compare the art of healing with a work of art, which from different standpoints and under different lighting reveals ever new and surprising beauty."

Another example of a laureate whose innovative work almost destroyed his career is Subramanyan Chandrasekhar (Physics, 1983). Chandrasekhar's life was marked by privilege and success. He suffered, however, one devastating blow which he nevertheless survived and over which he eventually triumphed.

Subramanyan Chandrasekhar was born in 1910 in Lahore, now in Pakistan but at that time in India, where his father worked as a government auditor. His mother was a translator, a gifted woman who was ambitious for her children. His uncle was C. V. Raman who won the Nobel Prize in physics in 1930. Chandrasekhar received his elementary education at home and attended the Presidency College in Madras, where he studied physics. In 1930 he went to Cambridge on an Indian government scholarship, where he earned his Ph.D. and was elected a fellow of Trinity College.

Chandrasekhar's personal bearing, like his physics, was invariably modest, elegant, and precise. On the sea voyage to England, and at Cambridge, he used quantum physics to calculate that a star of mass greater than 1.44 times that of the sun (subsequently named the Chandrasekhar limit) had to end its life by collapsing into an object of enormous density: what is now known as a black hole.

Chandrasekhar presented his theory at a meeting of the Royal Astronomical Society in 1935. Present at the meeting was Sir Arthur Eddington, the most distinguished British astrophysicist of the time, whom Chandrasekhar much admired, and, with whom, he had been in frequent contact. At the meeting, Eddington ridiculed Chandrasekhar's theory, saying "I think there should be a law of Nature to prevent a star from behaving in this absurd way!" Eddington believed that stars ended their lives as earth-sized lumps of metal called white dwarves.

This attack devastated Chandrasekhar. Although supportive in private, none of his colleagues came publicly to his defense. He went back over his calculations but could find no error. He changed the focus of his research from stellar structure to stellar dynamics, and in 1937 he left Cambridge, first for Harvard, and then for the University of Chicago, where he spent the rest of his career. He was the first nonwhite person appointed to the faculty of the University of Chicago. He edited the *Astrophysical Journal* for nineteen years. Two of his students at Chicago, Tsung-Dao Lee and Chen Ning Yang, won the Nobel Prize for Physics in 1957. Eddington died in 1944, having never retracted his attack on Chandrasekhar, in fact he continued to refer to Chandrasekhar's ideas as "stellar buffoonery."

Remarkably, Chandrasekhar maintained friendly relations with Eddington; in later years, he kept a portrait of Eddington on the wall of his office. Chandrasekhar's theory was eventually validated, he published a book on black holes, and he was awarded the Nobel Prize for Physics in 1983. Eddington's flippant remarks had delayed the work of science in this area by forty years. Chandrasekhar's attitude toward the controversy is perhaps best summed up in his own words: "I think one could say that a certain modesty toward understanding nature is a precondition to the continued pursuit of science"

Chandrasekhar was a victim of peer review. The astronomer Hannes Alfvén (Physics, 1970) remarked that:

> The peer review system is satisfactory during quiescent times, but not during a revolution in a discipline such as astrophysics, when the establishment seeks to preserve the status quo.

The same opinion was expressed somewhat differently by Luis Alvarez (Physics 1968): "I'm convinced that a controlled disrespect for authority is essential to a scientist." Linus Pauling expressed the same view:

> When an old and distinguished person speaks to you, listen to him carefully and with respect—but do not believe him. Never put your trust in anything but your own intellect.

The Peace Prize is not an exception, at least not in all cases, to the rule that Nobel laureates doggedly pursue a novel or unpopular course. Yitzhak Rabin (1994) and Anwar Al-Sadat (1978) both suffered assassination for their work for peace, as did Martin Luther King.

Hermann Hesse (Literature, 1946) wrote,

I have never been attacked or spat upon for any stupid, insignificant, worthless thing I have done; every time I have been reviled it has been for a thought or action that proved to be right.

Most writers experience rejection in their early careers, especially if their writing is unconventional. In the case of Samuel Beckett, this rejection went on for many years. Beckett ended his life famous and wealthy. But he achieved this status only after decades of obscurity and poverty.

Beckett was born into a middle-class Protestant family in Dublin, Ireland, in 1906. His father was a surveyor, and his mother had worked as a nurse. At school, he excelled in cricket; he later played for Dublin University. He enjoyed tennis, boxing, swimming, high diving, and distance running. He also played the piano, and was an enthusiastic bridge and chess player. He graduated from Trinity College, Dublin, in 1927 with a degree in English, French, and Italian, then taught in Ireland and lectured at the École Normal Supérieur in Paris. He taught French at Trinity College until 1931, when he resigned to devote himself to writing. He moved to Paris, where he became friendly with James Joyce. He published his first work in 1929, a critical essay largely in defense of Joyce. In 1931 he published a study of Proust.

After his father's death, he received a small annuity. He lived in London from 1933 to 1936, where he underwent psychoanalysis, the cost of which was underwritten by his mother. His first work of fiction, a collection of short stories, was published in 1934, to critical bewilderment and dismal sales. In 1935, a collection of his poems was published in an edition of 327 copies. Perpetually broke, he would periodically return home to Ireland. In 1933-37 he spent several months in Germany, and then moved to France. He was now competent in German, and fluent in French and Italian. His novel Murphy was published in 1938, after being rejected by numerous publishers. It brought him neither fame nor fortune. He became involved with a number of women, including the American heiress Peggy Guggenheim. In Paris in 1938, he suffered a near-fatal stab wound to the chest in an unprovoked attack by a pimp.

He was in Ireland when war broke out, but went to Paris, saying he preferred France at war to Ireland at peace. He joined the Resistance in August 1941, his role being to collate and deliver reports of German military activities. But the Resistance cell was betrayed, and Beckett and his partner Suzanne had to go into hiding. Eventually they settled in

Roussillon, a small village in the south of France. They lived in great poverty, Beckett working for local farmers in exchange for food. He continued to help the Resistance by hiding arms and explosives. At the end of the war, he was awarded the Croix de Guerre and the Medaille de la Reconnaissance Française.

Beckett's writings after the war were written in French, which he claimed enabled him to write "without style". He translated them into English himself. With the end of the German occupation, Beckett moved back to Paris. Post-war inflation rendered his financial situation dire; he earned a little money from translations and reviews. As a writer he was still essentially unknown. His novels *Molloy and Malone Dies* had difficulty finding publishers, and sold very few copies.

The work that made Beckett famous was *Waiting for Godot*, written in the winter of 1948-1949. In this two-act play, two tramps meet near a bare tree on a country road. They are waiting for Godot, who never arrives. While waiting, they recall the past, eat, tell jokes, and speculate about Godot. The play was first produced in France, to considerable acclaim. Reaction was more mixed to the British production, but soon it was being produced throughout Europe and in the United States, putting an end to Beckett's years of poverty. Beckett's subsequent works, including Krapp's *Last Tape*, *Endgame*, *All that Fall*, and *Happy Days*, found a ready reception.

In 1961, Beckett married his long-time partner, Suzanne. When he received the Nobel Prize in 1961, Suzanne said it was a "catastrophe." Beckett declined to go to Stockholm for the award ceremony, and maintained his privacy by refusing almost all interviews. He gave much of the prize money away. He spent his time at his apartment in Rue St. Jacques, at the neighborhood café, and at his country cottage outside Paris. He continued to produce new work for the rest of his life, though his time was increasingly occupied by directing his plays for stage, film, and television. He died in 1989, at the age of 83.

Beckett is often considered a pessimist, yet he said, "When you are in the last bloody ditch, there is nothing left but to sing." and "Ever tried. Ever failed. No matter. Try Again. Fail again. Fail better."

Great discoveries are rarely made by people who are averse to risks. Embarking on a new area of research, challenging time-honored assumptions, parting company with established experts, writing in an unconventional way, all involve some degree of risk. One laureate who exemplifies this willingness to take risks is Roderick McKinnon

(Chemistry, 2003), who twice gave up a profitable career to follow his research instincts.

MacKinnon was born in 1956, the fourth of seven children in a family of modest means. He describes his home environment as follows:

> My parents provided a happy environment and made their expectations clear to us. Television is bad for you, reading is good for you, and you better get an A for effort in school. What you end up doing in life is up to you. Just make sure you enjoy what you do because then you will do it well.

From an early age, MacKinnon was always asking questions. He read books on geology and had collections of rocks, butterflies, snakes and other living things. He was allowed to take a microscope home from school and used it to examine everything he could find. Through high school he was a member of the gymnastics team. He began to study science seriously at Brandeis University, where he also met his wife.

Despite urging by his advisor to continue in science, he went on to medical school. He completed medical school in four years, and then spent a further three years in training. But the appeal of pure science was too strong, and despite having dedicated seven years to medicine, he returned to science during the end of his house officer training. By this time he was nearly 30, still earning a pittance, and being supported by his wife's employment. MacKinnon's ambition to do basic science was stimulated in part by the loss of his sister to leukemia. He was appointed to a position at Harvard, where he established a successful laboratory. But a further career change came when he was offered a position at Rockefeller University, which would enable him to specialize in studies of the atomic structure of K+ selectivity. Once again, he left a promising position to make a new start. At Rockefeller, he built another highly successful laboratory, and in 2003 was awarded the Nobel Prize for Medicine "for structural and mechanistic studies of ion channels."

In summarizing his experience, MacKinnon says,

> If you develop a fascination, hear a little voice inside telling you to take a road that was not anticipated, don't be afraid to listen to the voice and follow the road... What is most important is that you find your passion and pursue it... Just take a risk. Go for it. I

think if you crash and burn trying, it's still going to be better than if you never tried at all.

Chapter 14
Intelligence and Intuition

It would seem to be a truism to state that Nobel laureates are intelligent. But some Nobel laureates have questioned the role of intelligence in their success. Here is Rita Levi-Montalcini:

> In scientific research, neither the degree of one's intelligence, nor the ability to carry out one's tasks with thoroughness and precision are factors essential to personal success and fulfillment. More important... are total dedication and a tendency to underestimate difficulties, which cause one to tackle problems that other, more critical and acute persons instead opt to avoid.

Glenn Seaborg:

> All my life I've been surrounded by people who are smarter than I am, but I found I could always keep up by working hard.

Richard Feynman:

> I don't know a great deal. I have a limited intelligence, and I use it in a particular direction.

Albert Einstein:

> I have no special talents. I am only passionately curious.

John Bardeen, who won the Nobel Prize for Physics in 1956 and again in 1972, argued that "You can't measure intelligence by IQ or any other single number. There are many different kinds of intelligence." Many psychologists would agree. The psychologist J. P. Guilford spent much of his 90-year life studying intelligence. Working in the US Army Air Corps in World War II, he identified 25 ability factors, the use of which in pilot selection resulted in a reduction of the failure rate in pilot training by two-thirds. The final version of his theory represented intelligence as consisting of 180 distinct abilities. Howard Gardner proposed that there are seven main types of intelligence: logical-mathematical, linguistic, musical, spatial, bodily-kinesthetic, interpersonal, and intrapersonal. More recently, the concept of emotional intelligence has gained ground. Self-perceived ability is another factor to be taken into account. These various facets of intelligence do not correlate highly with one another, nor does any one of them independently predict achievement very well. Intelligence test scores cease to be predictive at higher levels. As Mihaly Csikszentmihalyi puts it: "After a certain point, IQ does not seem to be correlated any longer with superior performance in real life."

Logical and deductive reasoning is critical to the work of Nobel laureates. But, also important, are what might be considered three other varieties of intelligence: creativity, imagination, and intuition. According to Csikszentmihalyi:

> a genuinely creative accomplishment is almost never the result of a sudden insight, a light bulb flashing on in the dark, but comes after years of hard work.

Creative people often refer to an intuitive sense that guides them, pointing to the difference between intuition and logical-deductive reasoning. Roy Glauber (Physics, 2005) said:

> Too many kids in school get the notion that science is deductive. And deductive science is almost never creative. Real ideas come via intuition, via guesswork, and we're guessing all the time.

Here is an excerpt from Ralph Moss's biography of Albert Szent-Gyorgyi (Medicine, 1937):

> It was around this time that Albert first recognized what he referred to as his "special gift." This was his intuitive ability to look at a problem and divine, if not the solution, then the correct question to ask. It was almost as if he could speak directly to nature, "hear her voice," as he later put it, and translate that feeling into action. This almost mystical feeling, akin to a poet's or artist's inspiration, was to remain the basis of his "scientific method" for the rest of his life.

Eric Kandel (Medicine, 2000) felt rather similarly:

> There are many situations in which one cannot decide on the basis of cold facts alone—because facts are often insufficient. One ultimately has to trust one's unconscious, one's instincts, one's creative urge.

Einstein spoke of "a feeling of direction" that guided his investigations. He also said, "A new idea comes suddenly and in a rather intuitive way," but he added, "But, intuition is nothing but the outcome of earlier intellectual experience." Einstein once had a discussion with the poet St. John Perse (Literature, 1960). He asked Perse: "How does the idea of a poem come?" And Perse spoke of the role of intuition and imagination. "It is the same for the man of science," Einstein replied:

> It is a sudden illumination--almost a rapture. Later to be sure, intelligence analyzes and experiments confirm or invalidate the intuition. But initially there is a great forward leap of the imagination.

Michael Brown (Medicine 1985) said

> As we did our work, I think, we almost felt at times that there was almost a hand guiding us, because we could go from one step to the next, and somehow we would know which was the right way to go.

Similarly, Stanley Cohen (Medicine, 1986) said: "I am not always right, but I do have feelings about what is an important observation and what is probably trivial." George Stigler (Economics, 1982) said, "I consider that I have good intuition and good judgment on what problems are worth pursuing and what lines of work are worth doing." Csikszentmihalyi, in his study of ten Nobel laureates, cites Manfed Eigen (Chemistry, 1967) as one of several laureates who asserted that the difference between themselves and less creative colleagues was that they could tell whether a problem was soluble or not.

Rita Levi-Montalcini (Medicine, 1986) once remarked:

I have no particular intelligence, just average intelligence [but] something comes into my mind, and I know it's true. It is a particular gift in the subconscious. In the night it happens… it's not rational. You've been thinking about something without willing to for a long time… Then, all of a sudden, the problem is opened to you in a flash, and you suddenly see the answer.

Leon Lederman also spoke of the sudden realization that:

usually happens at three in the morning. Suddenly, you become aware of a fact or a process that no one on the planet knows. You've learned something important. There are signs. Your palms sweat. You get chilled… It may not happen often. Maybe once in your life. But it's unbeatable.

Ference Marton, Peter Fensham, and Seth Chaiklin reviewed interviews with Nobel laureates in science conducted by the Swedish Broadcasting Service from 1970 to 1986 to determine what position they took on the question of intuition. Their conclusion:

Practically all laureates consider scientific intuition to be distinctly different from conscious, logical reasoning processes, and to concern the direction of research, more often the finding of a path than reaching the goal. The experience of intuition is frequently characterized as having a certitude based on a feeling or a perception of almost aesthetic or quasi-sensory nature. Scientific intuition seems to develop through extended and varied experiences of the object of research and is apparently based on an initially vague, global, not fully conscious, anticipatory perception of the solution searched for; a simultaneous grasp of the whole, well in advance of knowing its parts in detail.

Intuition, it seems, is not some mysterious quality that is an innate characteristic of genius. Nor is it simply a matter of paying attention to gut feelings. It is rather a sharpening of perception that is usually the product of long-term immersion in the varied data and methodologies of the field of endeavor.

In describing their own work, writers tend to eschew the words creativity, intuition, and inspiration. They are more likely to stress the hard work entailed in creating prose and poetry. Derek Walcott (Literature, 1992) said simply, "Poetry, I think, is the toughest bloody art in the world."

In an article for *Esquire* in 1934, Hemingway wrote:

> The hardest thing in the world to do is to write straight honest prose on human beings. First you have to know the subject; then you have to know how to write. Both take a lifetime to learn.

Twenty years later, he returned to this theme:

> Fiction, prose rather, is possibly the roughest trade of all in writing. You do not have the reference, the old important reference. You have the sheet of blank paper, the pencil, and the obligation to invent truer than things can be true.

The belief that creative artists merely follow the promptings of inspiration is one that is explicitly rejected by writers.

Joseph Brodsky said:

> Seen from the outside, creativity is the object of fascination or envy; seen from within it is an unending exercise in uncertainty and a tremendous school for insecurity.

Anatole France (Literature, 1921) spoke for many when he said, "I do not believe that there is poetry without art nor art without craftsmanship."

Roald Hoffmann, who won the Nobel Prize for chemistry in 1981, is also an active and published poet. He says:

> I think poetry and a lot of science are creation. They're acts of creation that are accomplished with craftsmanship--an intensity, with a concentration, a detachment, an economy of statement.

Konrad Lorenz (Medicine, 1973) would have agreed:

> He who has once seen the intimate beauty of nature cannot tear himself away from it again. He must become either a poet or a naturalist, and, if his eyes are good and his powers of observation sharp enough, he may well become both.

Wislawa Szymborska (Literature, 1996) is one of the few poets to speak directly of inspiration. She claimed that:

> Inspiration is not the exclusive privilege of poets or artists generally. There is, has been, and will always be a certain group of people whom inspiration visits. It's made up of all those who've consciously chosen their calling and do their job with love and imagination.

Can intuition and creativity be applied to the work of those men and women who have won the Nobel Peace Prize? Let us look at the work of Henri Dumont, who won the first Peace Prize in 1901.

Dunant was born in 1828 into a religious and humanitarian family in Geneva. As a young man he worked for the YMCA, travelling in France, Belgium, and Holland. At 26, he became a representative of a Geneva company operating in North Africa, and at 30 published his first book, on Tunis, which contained a chapter on slavery in Islamic countries and the United States. Dunant next established a company, capitalized at 100,000,000 francs, to exploit a large tract of land in Algeria. Unable to obtain water rights, he decided to take his appeal directly to Emperor Napoleon III. At that time, Napoleon was commanding the French armies, who, with their Italian allies, were endeavouring to drive the Austrians out of Italy. It was thus that Dunant arrived at Solferino, in northern Italy, in 1859, in time to witness the battle and its aftermath.

Solferino was one of the bloodiest battles of the era. When the fighting was over, along with the corpses of men and horses, thousands of soldiers lay wounded on the battlefield, without medical aid, water, or rescue. Military medical services were rudimentary. There were few medicines, bandages, surgeons, or nurses. Dunant helped to organize local people to carry the wounded to churches in local villages and nurse them there. He spent his own money on supplies and pressed into service passing tourists from France and Britain.

He published an account of his experiences in a small book, *A Memory of Solferino*. The book made Dunant famous. The royal courts of Europe sent him their congratulations. *A Memory of Solferino* contained a proposal that nations should form relief societies, and train volunteers, to care for the war-wounded. In 1863 the Geneva Society for Public Welfare appointed Dunant and four others to examine the possibility of putting this plan into action. The Committee called for an international conference, which Dunant travelled Europe to promote, and which was held in October 1863, with 39 delegates from 16 countries in attendance. The following year, 12 nations signed an international treaty, the Geneva Convention, agreeing to guarantee neutrality to sanitary personnel, to expedite supplies for their use, and to adopt a special identifying emblem—in virtually all instances a red cross on a field of white Thus began the Red Cross. Dunant wrote:

> Surely, if those who make the slaughter can claim a place on the roll of honor, those who cure, and cure often at the risk of their lives, are entitled to their due of esteem and gratitude.

Dunant continued his work by extending the scope of the Red Cross to cover naval personnel in wartime, and in peacetime to aid in natural catastrophes. He set out plans for the creation of a neutral colony in Palestine, and for an "International and Universal Library" of the great masterpieces of literature In 1872 he convened a conference to consider an international convention on the handling of prisoners of war and settling international disputes by courts of arbitration.

Meanwhile, in 1864, Dunant's company had gone into liquidation. Water rights were not granted, his cattle died of thirst, his company had been mismanaged, and he had given it insufficient attention. The court ordered the directors to make good the losses. Many Genevans had lost money, and Dunant became a social pariah. He offered to resign from the International Committee, and his offer was accepted with alacrity. Thenceforth, the International Committee belittled Dunant's contribution, and maligned him to other people. When a history of the Red Cross was published, it did not mention Dunant's name. This did not prevent Dunant from continuing his work, persuading the Shah of Persia, for example, to sign the Geneva Convention. He helped to found a

Universal Alliance for Order and Civilization, concerned with slavery and labor conditions, which soon became involved in promoting a convention to protect prisoners of war.

For the next twenty years, from 1875 to 1895, Dunant sank into obscurity. He wrote that there were times when he dined on a crust of bread, blackened his coat with ink, whitened his collar with chalk, and slept out of doors. After brief stays in various places, he settled down in Heiden, a small Swiss village. Because he was ill, Dunant was moved in 1892 to the hospice at Heiden. There, in Room 12, he spent the remaining eighteen years of his life, his tiny income provided by relatives. He spent much of his time in depression, deepened by feelings of persecution.

In 1895 a journalist sought Dunant out and a long interview resulted. Other newspapers picked up the interview, and the great and the good descended on Heiden to visit Dunant. In 1901, together with the French pacifist Plessy, he was awarded the Nobel Peace Prize. Dunant died in 1910 and was buried without ceremony. His prize money, which he had not spent, he bequeathed to charity.

Dunant's decision to involve himself in the care of the wounded after the Battle of Solferino was an immediate decision based on simple human compassion. His work in founding the Red Cross, though perhaps inspired, was not a momentary inspiration; but it was the product of months of travel and negotiation.

Examples could be drawn from the lives of many other Peace laureates. Willy Brandt (1971), Chancellor of West Germany, dropping to his knees when he visited Auschwitz. Martin Luther King, sitting alone in his cell and writing his Letter from Birmingham Jail in the margins of a newspaper. Betty Williams and Mairead Corrigan (1976) reacting to the sudden death of three small children in Northern Ireland by starting the Women for Peace movement. Mohammad Yunus (2006) lending $27 to 42 poor village women in Bangladesh who had become victims of a local moneylender, and thus starting the Grameen Bank, which by 2008 had disbursed $6.6 billion in small loans to Asia's poor.

Albert Schweitzer (Peace, 1952) described how he realized the key to his philosophy:

> Late on the third day, at the very moment when, at sunset, we were making our way through a herd of hippopotamuses, there flashed upon my mind, unforeseen and unsought, the phrase, "Reverence

for Life" The iron door had yielded: the path in the thicket had become visible.

But, like the prizes for literature and science, the Nobel Peace Prize is not awarded for a momentary inspiration, but for the hard and sometimes dangerous work that is conducted year after year to make of the inspiration a new reality.

Chapter 15
The Happiest People
on the Planet

Prosaic as it may be, hard work plays a major part in the success of Nobel laureates. But for this group of men and women, their work is their delight.

Theodor Mommsen, who won the first Literature prize in 1901, said simply, "Without passion there is no genius."

James Cronin (Physics, 1980) remarked:

> When I ask myself, 'Who are the happiest people on the planet?' my answer is, 'Those who can't wait to wake up in the morning to get back to what they were doing the day before.'

Winston Churchill observed that "Those whose work and pleasure are one... are... Fortune's favoured children."

François Jacob:

> That one could live, travel, eat, and raise a family while spending the best part of one's time doing what one loves, that seemed like a miracle I still found hard to believe!

Joshua Lederberg advised students: "Try hard to find out what you're good at, and what your passions are, and where the two converge, and build your life around that."

Barry Marshall made a similar remark in his Nobel Acceptance speech:

> To young people listening tonight I would say, find passion in your work—whatever it is.... Work hard, keep balance in your life and, just in case, always be nice to Swedish people.

Richard Feynman gave similar advice:

Work hard to find something that fascinates you. When you find it you will know your lifework... The man happy in his work is not the narrow specialist, nor the well-rounded man, but the man who is doing what he loves to do.

Rosalind Yalow agreed: "I had to work very hard, but I did it because I wanted to. That's the real key to happiness."

Leon Lederman said,

You have to know what makes you happy, what makes you say "Thank God it's Monday," instead of "Thank God it's Friday." You're going to spend some vast fraction of your life in your business, whatever it is, whether it's running a lathe, running a corporation, or running an experiment. Therefore, you want to really enjoy it, otherwise it's a dumb thing you're going to do.

At the age of 81, Barbara McClintock said: "I never thought of stopping, and I just hated sleeping. I can't imagine having a better life." Barry Sharpless (Economics, 2001) probably spoke for many laureates when he declared that "Passion, not planning, is the engine driving all my thought and action."

Albert Einstein was even more succinct: "Work. There is nothing else." John Steinbeck (Literature, 1962) agreed: "Work is the only good thing." Ernest Hemingway felt the same: "To work was the only thing, it was the one thing that always made you feel good." Pablo Neruda (Literature, 1971) made a similar point: "For me writing is like breathing. I could not live without breathing and I could not live without writing."

The lives of the Nobel Peace laureates tend to confirm this pattern. Rigoberta Menchu Tum (Peace, 1992) said:

My life does not belong to me. I've decided to offer it to a cause. They can kill me at any time, but let it be when I'm fulfilling a mission, so I'll know that my blood will not be shed in vain, but will serve as an example to my *compañeros*.

On this point we have near, but not complete unanimity. Subrahmanyan Chandrasekhar was one scientist who expressed some reservations about a life entirely dedicated to science:

It does not seem to me that the pursuit of science results in the feeling of contentment or peace after years of pursuit... It's not at all clear to me whether the single-minded pursuit of science at the expense of other, personal aspects of one's life is justifiable.

Chapter 16
Grace under Pressure

The lives of Nobel laureates suggest that courage and genius are associated. To challenge tradition and orthodoxy by making new discoveries, by writing in a new way, or by speaking out on behalf of peace or freedom, requires moral courage. Courage and integrity are additionally tested when the individual is the subject of an oppressive regime. Such was the case of Albert Lutuli in South Africa during the apartheid era.

Albert Lutuli was born in or about 1898 in Rhodesia and grew up in Natal, South Africa. His grandfather and uncle were chiefs of their tribe; his father was a Christian missionary. He was educated at mission schools, and earned a teaching certificate in 1917. He worked as a teacher and teacher educator for many years, and was elected president of the African Teachers Association in 1933. He was also active in church work, becoming a lay reader and an executive member of the Christian Council of South Africa. He married a fellow teacher, and they had seven children. In 1936 he gave up the security of teaching to accept the position of chief of his tribe, and devoted himself to the welfare of its 5000 members. This position combined the roles of magistrate, mediator, presiding dignitary, and representative of the central government.

In 1948, the Nationalist Party adopted the policy of apartheid, and in the 1950s enacted many laws, including the Pass Laws, restricting the rights of non-whites in South Africa. In 1944, Lutuli joined the African National Congress, becoming president of the Natal Division of the ANC in 1951. In 1952 he helped organize nonviolent protests against the discriminatory laws. The government demanded that he give up his membership in the ANC, and when he refused, dismissed him from his position as chief. In his public statement, Lutuli said:

> What the future has in store for me I do not know. It might be ridicule, imprisonment, concentration camp, flogging, banishment and even death. I only pray to the Almighty to strengthen my resolve so that none of these grim possibilities may deter me from striving, for the sake of the good name of our beloved country, the

Union of South Africa, to make it a true democracy and a true union in form and spirit of all the communities in the land.

Shortly thereafter, Lutuli was elected President-General of the African National Congress. The government banned him from public meetings for two years, and when this period expired, banned him from traveling more than twenty miles from his home. Such bans amounted to internal exile. After this ban expired, he attended an ANC conference in 1956, and was arrested and charged with treason with 155 others. He was held in custody, but was released after a year and the charges were dropped. He was next banned for five years from publishing and from travelling more than fifteen miles from his home. In 1960, he was arrested for publicly burning his pass following the "Sharpeville Massacre," in which 69 protestors against the pass laws were killed by South African police. Despite his persecution by the government, Lutuli emphasized the importance of not defining himself as a victim. "The tendency to see oneself perpetually as a victim will lead to the evasion of responsibility and the condoning of evil."

In 1961, Albert Lutuli was awarded the Nobel Peace Prize; the government temporarily lifted the ban to allow him to travel to Oslo. In his Nobel lecture, he said:

> To remain neutral in a situation where the laws of the land virtually criticized God for having created men of color was the sort of thing I could not, as a Christian, tolerate.

On its expiry, the five-year ban was renewed. In July 1967, he was struck by a freight train and killed as he walked over a trestle bridge near his home.

In answer to a question by Marlene Dietrich, Ernest Hemingway defined courage as "grace under pressure." Such grace was shown by Andrei Sakharov (Physics, 1975), one of the Soviet Union's leading scientists, who suffered years of persecution and internal exile for his political beliefs.

Sakharov was born in Moscow in 1921, son of a teacher of physics. He wrote of his home:

> The house was pervaded by a strong traditional family spirit—a vital enthusiasm for work and respect for professional competence. Within the family we provided one another with mutual support, just as we shared a love of literature and science.

He entered Moscow State University in 1938, moving with it when it was evacuated to Turkmenistan in 1941. During the war he worked for a time as a lumberjack and in a munitions factory. He also began to write scientific articles. He returned to Moscow in 1945 to study at the Physical Institute of the Soviet Academy of Sciences, earning his Ph.D. in 1947, with a dissertation on nuclear physics.

He worked on the Soviet atom bomb which was first tested in 1949, and then on the development of the hydrogen bomb, which was tested in 1953. In that year he was awarded the D.Sc. degree, elected to the Soviet Academy of Sciences, and awarded the title Hero of Socialist Labor. He continued to work on development of the hydrogen bomb; in 1961 a 50 megaton device was tested, the most powerful ever exploded. He also developed ideas for nuclear fusion, and advanced other initiatives in theoretical physics and cosmology. He opposed nuclear proliferation and supported the 1963 Treaty banning atmospheric tests of nuclear weapons. During this period, Sakharov began to nurture doubts about the political and biological implications of the nuclear arms race.

In 1967 Sakharov wrote to the Soviet leadership urging it to accept an American proposal to reject the development of antiballistic missile defense. The government ignored the letter and did not give permission for him to publish it. In 1968 he completed his *Progress, Peaceful Coexistence and Intellectual Freedom*. This essay circulated in samizdat prior to being published abroad. As a consequence, Sakharov was banned from military-related research. In 1970 he cofounded the Moscow Human Rights Committee. His first wife having died, he married a fellow human rights activist, Yelena Bonner in 1972. He was awarded the Nobel Peace Prize in 1975, but was not allowed to go to Oslo to receive it.

Sakharov remained under political pressure after winning the Nobel Prize. He was arrested following his public protests against the Soviet invasion of Afghanistan, and sent into exile in the closed city of Gorky. He was kept under close police surveillance, and several of his friends were arrested. "Yet, even so," he wrote, "both now and for always, I intend to hold fast to my belief in the hidden strength of the human spirit."

This period ended when Mikhail Gorbachev (Peace, 1990) instituted his policies of perestroika and glasnost. Sakharov was elected to parliament in 1989, but died the same year of a heart attack. He was at the time preparing a challenge to the Soviet government to extend democracy, and his last words were, "Tomorrow there will be a battle."

One of the great documents of the struggle for human rights is the *Letter from Birmingham Jail* by Martin Luther King. King was jailed four times for his civil rights activities. He was co-leading the movement in Birmingham, Alabama in April 1963 when he was arrested for leading an illegal demonstration. His letter was an impassioned statement of principle addressed to leading Birmingham churchmen, who had publicly opposed his campaign:

> I have almost reached the regrettable conclusion that the Negro's great stumbling block in his stride toward freedom is not the White Citizen's Councillor or the Ku Klux Klanner, but the white moderate... Shallow understanding from people of good will is more frustrating than absolute misunderstanding from people of ill will. Lukewarm acceptance is much more bewildering than outright rejection.

King was born in 1929, the son of a Baptist pastor. He skipped the ninth and twelfth grade and left high school at 15 without formally graduating. At 19 he received his BA in sociology from Morehouse College in Atlanta. He was ordained a minister at eighteen. He said:

> I'm the son of a preacher... my grandfather was a preacher, my great-grandfather was a preacher, my only brother is a preacher, my daddy's brother is a preacher, so I didn't have much choice.

He then spent three years studying for his B.D. degree at Crozier Theological College in Pennsylvania, graduating in 1951. He enrolled in graduate studies in systematic theology at Boston University, and received his doctorate in 1955. He met his wife Coretta, who was from Alabama, in Boston, with whom he had two sons and two daughters.

In 1954, at the age of 25, Martin Luther King was appointed pastor of the Dexter Avenue Baptist Church in Montgomery, Alabama. He was now a member of the executive committee of the National Association for the Advancement of Colored People. When the bus boycott began in Montgomery in December 1955, he accepted leadership of the movement, becoming a national figure. A year later the courts declared laws requiring segregation on buses unconstitutional. During the boycott, King was arrested and his home was bombed.

In 1957, King was elected president of the Southern Christian Leadership Conference, an organization formed to provide new leaders for the civil rights movement. Its principles were based on the Gospels and the works of Gandhi. King visited India and the family of Mahatma Gandhi in 1959. Over the next decade, he traveled six million miles, spoke over 2500 times, and wrote five books and numerous articles. While signing one of his books in 1958, he barely escaped death when he was stabbed by a demented Black woman. One of the major protests against segregation that he led was in Birmingham, Alabama. Sit-ins and marches were organized, and a large number of children were recruited for what became known as the "children's crusade." The Birmingham police responded with water cannon and police dogs. While imprisoned, King wrote his "Letter from Birmingham Jail."

In 1963, King led the March on Washington, to which he delivered his "I have a dream" speech:

> I have a dream that one day on the red hills of Georgia the sons of former slaves and the sons of former slave owners will be able to sit down together at a table of brotherhood. I have a dream that one day even the state of Mississippi, a desert state, sweltering with the heat of injustice and oppression, will be transformed into an oasis of freedom and justice. I have a dream that my four little children will one day live in a nation where they will not be judged by the color of their skin but by the content of their character... With this faith we will be able to work together, to pray together, to struggle together, to go to jail together, to stand up for freedom together, knowing that we will be free one day.

During his career, King was arrested more than twenty times and assaulted at least four times. In 1963 *Time Magazine* named him Man of the Year. J. Edgar Hoover, Director of the FBI, suspicious of communist influence in the civil rights movement, began tapping King's phones in 1963. When no evidence of communist infiltration appeared, the FBI kept audio files of King's extramarital affairs, and later endeavored to use them to pressure King to give up his work for civil rights.

In 1964, King became the youngest person up to that time to receive the Nobel Peace Prize. He donated the prize money to the civil rights movement. The Civil Rights Act of 1964 and the Voting Rights Act of 1965 realized many of the goals of the movement. In 1965, King, who had previously supported President Johnson, began to criticize the Vietnam War, both on political grounds and because it diverted funds from social programs. This lost him some support in the mainstream media.

In April 1968, King was assassinated in Memphis, Tennessee. He was posthumously awarded the Presidential Medal of Freedom in 1977 and the Congressional Gold Medal in 2004. More than 750 cities in the United States have streets named after King. Martin Luther King Day was established on the third Monday of January as a US national holiday in 1986. In his last speech, the night before his death, Martin Luther King delivered his own epitaph:

> I don't know what will happen now. We've got some difficult days ahead. But it doesn't matter with me now. Because I've been to the mountaintop and I don't mind. Like anybody, I would like to live a long life. Longevity has its place. But I'm not concerned about that now. I just want to do God's will. And he's allowed me to go up to the mountain. And I've looked over. And I've seen the Promised Land. I may not get there with you. But I want you to know tonight, that we, as a people, will get to the Promised Land. And I'm happy, tonight. I'm not worried about anything. I'm not fearing any man. Mine eyes have seen the glory of the coming of the Lord.

The motive to lend protection to a champion of human rights may have influenced the selection of Shirin Ebadi for the Nobel Peace prize in 2003. The Prize followed years of arrests, imprisonment, and personal danger.

Shirin Ebadi was born in 1947 in Iran to a family of academics and practising Muslims, filled with kindness and affection. Shirin gained admission to the Faculty of Law at Tehran University in 1965, and began to serve as a judge in 1969, the first woman in Iran to do so. She obtained her doctorate in law in 1971.

Following the Islamic Revolution in 1979, Shirin and other women judges were dismissed and given clerical duties. She resigned, but was not allowed to set up her own law practice until 1992. During this period of forced inactivity she wrote several books and articles. In her writing and her law practice she defended victims of conservative attack and repression, including homosexuals, members of the Baha'i community, and the families of intellectuals murdered by employees of the Iranian Ministry of Intelligence. She cofounded the Human Rights Defence Centre and the Society for Protecting the Rights of the Child, and lectured widely on Human Rights in Iran and abroad. For these activities she was imprisoned in the notorious Evin Prison, interrogated for hours, blindfolded, kicked, and given contaminated water to drink.

Shirin Ebadi says, "When I'm about to go to prison, one of the first things I do is to make enough food and put it in the fridge for my family." She espouses an interpretation of Islam that is in harmony with equality and democracy. Her practical good sense is illustrated by her remark that "Instead of telling girls to cover their hair, we should teach them to use their heads." She opposes the idea of emigration or of foreign intervention in Iran's affairs. The risks that she ran, and continues to run, are vividly indicated in the following passage from her 2006 book, *Iran Awakening*:

> I had reached... the transcript of a conversation between a government minister and a member of the death squad. When my eyes first fell on the sentence that would haunt me for years to come, I thought I had misread. I blinked once, but it stared back at me from the page: "The next person to be killed is Shirin Ebadi."

In 2003, Shirin Ebadi was awarded the Nobel Prize for Peace, "for her efforts for democracy and human rights... focused especially on the struggle for the rights of women and children." She stayed in Iran as long as she could: "I feel afraid, yes. But because I've worked in this field for so long, I've learnt to control my fear." But after continuing death threats, and the arrest and beating of her husband, in 2009 she left Iran to continue her work from abroad.

Chapter 17
Never Give In

The Nobel celebrations in Stockholm and Oslo last for a week, but the path to the prize is measured in years and decades. One of the most striking factors in the success of Nobel laureates is their capacity for perseverance.

When Hemingway was a young man, trying to support a wife and child while making his way as a writer living in Paris, he would sometimes be reduced to tears as his work was repeatedly rejected. But he persevered:

> Sometimes when I was starting a new story and I could not get it going... I would stand and look out over the roofs of Paris and think, "Do not worry. You have always written before and you will write now. All you have to do is write one true sentence. Write the truest sentence that you know."

The rejections, discouragement, and "writer's block" that are an inevitable part of the writer's life are overcome by those who feel they have no alternative. Speaking to students at the University of Wisconsin, Sinclair Lewis (Literature, 1930) told them:

> If you want fame, be a prize fighter or a movie star. If you write, write because you must write. Because you can't help it. Write what you believe, what you know, what moves you. And always write the best you can. Be self-proud. You can fool the critics but never yourself. Remember you're competing with the best that's ever been written. Try to be better than the best. There's no limit for you and there can be no writing but great writing.

Elie Wiesel (Peace, 1986) gave similar advice:

> I'd also say to a young writer, if you can choose not to write, don't. Nothing is as painful; from the outside, people think it's good; it's

easy; it's romantic. Not at all. It's much easier not to write than to write. Except if you are a writer. Then you have no choice.

Alva Myrdal, who worked for years in the discouraging area of disarmament during the Cold War, said this:

> I have, despite all disillusionment, never, never allowed myself to feel like giving up. This is my message today; it is not worthy of a human being to give up. We win nothing by doing only wishful thinking. There is always something one can do.

Nobel Prize winners are no more immune from hard times than the rest of humanity. It is instructive to see how they deal with difficulties and with tragedy.

Although Winston Churchill's life climaxed with his leadership of Britain in World War II, he experienced periods of rejection, when his reputation was shattered and his voice ignored.

Churchill was born in 1874 into a family of privilege; his father was Chancellor of the Exchequer, and his cousin was the Duke of Marlborough. Following school, he joined the army as a cavalry officer. He served in India, and then the Sudan, where he narrowly escaped death at the Battle of Omdurman in 1898. He joined the British forces in South Africa as a newspaper correspondent during the Boer War, was captured, and escaped. He returned to Britain and was almost immediately elected a Member of Parliament at the age of 26.

The beginning of the First World War found Churchill as First Lord of the Admiralty. Trench warfare produced a stalemate on the Western Front, where thousands of lives would be sacrificed for a few yards gained. "Are there no other alternatives than sending our armies to chew barbed wire in Flanders?" Churchill asked. He believed that an attack on Turkey, which was allied with Germany, would expose the southern flank of the Central Powers and relieve pressure in the West. But the attack on the Dardanelles was a disaster. The British troops were pinned down on the coast, disease became rampant, the British incurred over 200,000 casualties, and eventually the expeditionary force was withdrawn. It looked as if Churchill's political career was finished. He resigned from the cabinet and joined the army in France as a colonel. He returned to office at the end of the war and served as Chancellor of the Exchequer 1924-1929.

Throughout the 1930s, Churchill was out of office and out of favor. He spoke frequently in and outside of Parliament, about the hostile intentions of Hitler's Germany, and its growing strength, particularly in the air. His was a lonely voice, scoffed at by the complacent Conservative government. It was only in 1938, as the danger became too apparent to be ignored, that his warnings began to be taken seriously. When Chamberlain sold out Czechoslovakia to obtain a temporary peace with Hitler, Churchill said, "We have sustained a total and unmitigated defeat."

War broke out on 1 September 1939 when Germany attacked Poland. Churchill was appointed to his old position in charge of the Navy. Chamberlain lost the confidence of his party and resigned in May 1940. The choice of his successor came down to Churchill or Lord Halifax, who probably would have sued for peace with Hitler. Fortunately for Western Civilization, Churchill was chosen. At the end of the day, his bodyguard wished him success in his great task

:

> He said gravely, "God alone knows how great it is. All I hope is that it is not too late. I am very much afraid it is. We can only do our best." Tears came into his eyes. As he turned away, he muttered something to himself. Then he set his jaw, and with a look of determination, mastering all emotion, he began to climb the stairs.

Churchill's voice stiffened the backbone of the British through the dark days when the island stood alone against the might of Nazi Germany. Through the trials of the Dunkirk evacuation, the Battle of Britain, the Blitz, the campaign in North Africa, and the Normandy landings, Churchill's message was unfaltering:

> We shall not flag or fail. We shall go on to the end. We shall fight in France, we shall fight on the seas and oceans, we shall fight with growing confidence and growing strength in the air, we shall defend our island, whatever the cost may be. We shall fight on the beaches, we shall fight on the landing grounds, we shall fight in the fields and in the streets, we shall fight in the hills; we shall never surrender.

In 1941 he repeated the tone of defiance in a speech at his old school, Harrow:

> Never give in, never give in, never, never, never, never—in nothing, great or small, large or petty—never give in except to convictions of honor and good sense. Never yield to force; never yield to the apparently overwhelming might of the enemy.

The election of 1945, held after Germany's surrender, produced a Labour landslide. This is how Churchill described the event in the penultimate paragraph of the first volume of his history of the Second World War:

> Thus, then, on the night of the tenth of May [1940], at the outset of this mighty battle, I acquired the chief power in the State, which henceforth I wielded in ever-growing measure for five years and three months of world war, at the end of which time, all our enemies having surrendered unconditionally or being about to do so, I was immediately dismissed by the British electorate from all further conduct of their affairs.

At first cast into depression, he rallied and took on the task of leader of the opposition with vigor. He also used the time in opposition to write his history of the Second World War, the book that sealed his reputation as a writer. He was returned to office by the electorate in 1951, finally retiring in 1955.

Much admired in Scandinavia for his wartime service, Churchill was awarded the Nobel Prize for Literature in 1953. He was in fact a professional writer, and, not having inherited wealth, made his living from his pen during his entire career. He wrote some 40 books, several of which, including *My Early Life*, and his *History of the Second World War*, became instant classics. His achievements are the more remarkable in that, throughout his life, whenever he was not active, he struggled with depression, which he called his "black dog". He continued as a Member of Parliament into his 80s, and died in 1965 at the age of 91. In his last major speech in the House Commons, in 1955, he stated his philosophy in six words: "Never flinch, never weary, never despair."

Another politician who turned defeat to good account was President Carter. President Theodore Roosevelt (Peace, 1906) and President Woodrow Wilson (Peace, 1919) were both awarded the Nobel Peace Prize for contributions to world peace that they made while in office. Jimmy Carter was the first American politician to be awarded the prize for work undertaken after his Presidency. The story is one of triumph over the heartbreak and depression of political defeat.

Jimmy Carter was born in 1924 in Plains, Georgia, son of a farmer and a registered nurse. He was educated in local schools and at the US Naval Academy. He rose to lieutenant in the nuclear submarine service, but resigned from the navy on the death of his father and returned to Plains to manage the family business. The business prospered despite hostility in some quarters after Carter refused to subscribe to the White Citizens' Council. He won election to the Georgia senate in 1962 and as Governor of Georgia in 1970. He won the presidential election in 1976. The most significant success of his presidency was the Camp David Accords in September 1978. For thirteen days, Carter mediated between the representatives of Egypt and Israel, leading to a peace treaty between the two countries. Anwar Al-Sadat and Menachem Begin were awarded the Nobel Peace Prize for their role in the treaty, and it was widely felt that Carter should have been equally honored.

A major failure of Carter's presidency was the hostage crisis in Iran. When radicals seized the American embassy in Teheran on November 4, 1979, Carter chose negotiation over the immediate application of force, which was urged by many of his advisors. The humiliation of the US, and an abortive rescue attempt late in his presidency, helped Ronald Reagan defeat Carter in the 1976 election.

The failure to win a second term, and the reversal of most of his policies by the Reagan administration, were bitter blows to Jimmy Carter. After a period of reflection, Carter and his wife Rosalynn decided to devote themselves to the causes of peace and development. He founded the Carter Center in Atlanta, which has provided election observers at more than 70 elections in more than 20 countries. It has also worked to mediate conflicts between the United States and North Korea, between Cuba and the US, and within Haiti, Sudan, Ethiopia, Eritrea, Liberia, Nepal, Bosnia, and other countries.

The Carter Center has been heavily involved in health programs in Africa and South America. Guinea worm disease, a dreaded parasitic infection, has been reduced by 95 per cent. Over 100 million people have been treated for river blindness, and millions more for lymphatic filariasis, schistosomiasis, onchocerciasis, and trachoma, and millions of mosquito nets impregnated with insecticide have been distributed in malarial regions. The Centre has also been active in agriculture, enabling third world farmers to increase the productivity of their fields. The Carter Center has also been active in the field of human rights, drawing international attention to cases of violation, and working for the equality of women.

In all of his work, Carter's resolve has been strengthened by his religious faith:

> I have one life and one chance to make it count for something… My faith demands that I do whatever I can, wherever I am, whenever I can, for as long as I can with whatever I have to try to make a difference.

Jimmy Carter has lent his prestige to Habitat for Humanity, and he and his wife spend at least a week each year working on a Habitat Project. In this connection, he observes:

> My wife has never been more beautiful than when her face was covered with black smut from scraping burned ceiling joists, and streaked with sweat from carrying sheets of plywood.

In 2002, Jimmy Carter was awarded the Nobel Peace Prize. Asked on his seventieth birthday in 1994 what had been the best time of his life, he replied, "By far, my best years are those I'm enjoying now, since Rosalynn and I left the White House."

Theodore Roosevelt was another President who won the Nobel Prize. In a life marked by achievement and success, he experienced profound tragedy, the death of his wife and his mother on the same day.

Roosevelt was born in 1858 in New York. His wealthy family was descended from seventeenth century Dutch settlers. He showed an early interest in natural history, skinning and stuffing the birds he shot; he published a pamphlet on the birds of the Adirondacks when he was nineteen. He travelled widely with his family, developing facility in French and German. Suffering frequently from asthma and digestive troubles, he undertook rigorous exercise to strengthen his body. He attended Harvard, where he excelled in his studies and in sports, particularly boxing. His interest at this time was in becoming a scientist. He graduated *magna cum laude* in 1880 and the same year married Alice Lee. He attended Columbia Law School, but became disillusioned with the law after his first year. He then entered politics, being elected to the New York State Assembly, where he became known as a reformer. In 1882, his influential book, *The Naval War of 1812*, was published.

In 1884, he suffered a staggering blow when his wife and his mother both died, of different causes, on the same day. "The light has gone out of my life," he wrote in his diary. After completing the legislative term, he abandoned his political career and his home state, and moved to the badlands of Dakota Territory, where he purchased a ranch. The ranch was a financial failure, but during his two years as a rancher, Roosevelt became a big game hunter, captured outlaws, and experienced renewed health from the strenuous outdoor life. On his return to New York in 1886, he remarried, took a fifteen week honeymoon in Europe, and then returned to politics. He was appointed to the Civil Service Commission in Washington, but in 1895 he returned to New York to become President of the Board of Commissioners of the New York City Police Department. Here he undertook a purge of the notoriously corrupt and inefficient department. His work also gave him first-hand knowledge of how people lived in the slums of New York.

In 1897 he became Assistant Secretary of the Navy under President McKinley. In this office he worked hard to strengthen the United States Navy. When the war with Spain broke out in 1898, he resigned his office, and took the Lieutenant Colonelcy of a volunteer regiment largely composed of cowboys and hunters from the west, which quickly became known as the Rough Riders. Both Roosevelt and his regiment distinguished themselves in Cuba at the Battle of San Juan, and he returned to the States a national hero. Roosevelt, who had led the charge up San Juan Hill, was nominated for the Medal of Honor, but this was blocked by senior officers, whose inefficiency he had criticized. He was awarded the honor posthumously in 2001.

Roosevelt was elected governor of New York State in 1899. During his governorship, some thousand bills were made law, amongst other subjects promoting education and conservation, providing an eight-hour day for state workers, and cleaning up corruption. It was during this time that he coined the term, "the strenuous life."

I wish to preach, not the doctrine of ignoble ease but the doctrine of the strenuous life; the life of toil and effort; of labor and strife; to preach that highest form of success which comes, not to the man who desires more easy peace, but to the man who does not shrink from danger, from hardship, or from bitter toil, and who out of these wins the splendid ultimate triumph.

In 1900 he was chosen as vice-presidential candidate to McKinley, succeeding to the Presidency when McKinley was assassinated in 1901. He was the youngest president in US history. In 1904 Roosevelt was elected to a full term as President. During his presidency, he infuriated southerners by inviting the Black educator, Booker T. Washington, to dinner at the White House, he rooted out corruption in the civil service, he oversaw land redistribution in the Philippines, he presided over the secession of Panama from Columbia and started construction of the Panama Canal, he organized the irrigation of three million acres of farmland, he created five national parks, he renovated the White House, he settled the Alaska boundary dispute with Britain, he built up the US navy and reorganized the army and the national guard, and he expanded the Open Door policy with China. In 1905, he worked as a mediator between Russia and Japan, leading to the Treaty of Portsmouth, earning the Nobel Prize for Peace in 1906. He was the first American to win the Nobel Prize. Of his period in office, he was able to say:

When I left the Presidency, I finished seven and a half years of administration, during which not a shot had been fired against a foreign foe. We were at absolute peace, and there was no nation in the world... whom we had wronged, or from whom we had anything to fear.

William Howard Taft became President in 1909, but Roosevelt, initially Taft's supporter, decided to run against him in 1912, accepting nomination for the Progressive Party. At an election meeting, he was shot by a deranged man. The bullet passed through the papers he was holding, through a steel eyeglass case, and lodged against a rib, which it broke. Roosevelt delivered his speech before seeking medical attention. He received more votes than Taft, but Woodrow Wilson (Peace, 1919) outpolled both and became President. Roosevelt took a break from politics to go on safari in Africa, collecting specimens for the

Smithsonian Museum. During this safari he made 296 kills, including 9 lions, 13 rhinoceroses, 7 hippopotamuses, 8 elephants, 20 zebras, 6 buffaloes, and 7 giraffes.

In 1913, Roosevelt undertook a demanding journey of exploration in the area of the Amazon, during which he became severely ill. His health never fully recovered. With the outbreak of World War I, he urged intervention by the US. After the US entered the war, his youngest son, Quentin, was killed, to his great grief. Roosevelt died in January 1919, at the age of 60.

In addition to his other achievements, Roosevelt wrote 26 books, over a thousand magazine articles, as well as thousands of speeches and more than 150,000 letters.

A different order of hardship was experienced by Eugene O'Neill. At the age of 23, Eugene O'Neill was an unemployed sailor, living at Jimmy the Priest's rooming house in New York, an *habitué* of waterfront bars and whorehouses, broke all the time and drunk most of it. At the age of 48, he won the Nobel Prize for Literature.

O'Neill was born in New York City in 1888. His father was a well-known actor. After his birth, his mother became addicted to morphine. O'Neill's first seven years were spent touring with his father's company. The next ten years were spent at boarding schools. At 18, he entered Princeton, but left without completing his first year. Generally unemployed, dependent on his father for handouts, he nevertheless got married, and sired a son whom he never saw. He joined an expedition seeking gold in the jungles of Honduras, where he contracted malaria. In 1910, he signed on as crew on a Norwegian square-rigger. He left the ship in Buenos Aires, picked up odd jobs, became a beachcomber and a derelict. The following year he signed up on a British tramp steamer to South Africa. On returning to New York he settled in Jimmy the Priest's boarding house, and then sailed for Europe on the SS New York, returning on the SS Philadelphia. He was discharged with the rank of Able Seaman. He joined his father's acting troupe for a season. Back in New York, he drank steadily, including varnish and water and wood alcohol, made a half-hearted suicide attempt with Veronal, was divorced, worked as a reporter on the *New London Telegraph*, developed TB and made an extended stay at a sanatorium. These years of adventure and desperation provided O'Neill with material that would last for his entire playwriting career. Later, he was to write:

I don't love life because it is pretty. Prettiness is only clothes-deep. I am a truer lover than that. I love it naked. There is beauty to me even in its ugliness. In fact, I deny the ugliness entirely, for its vices are often nobler than its virtues.

O'Neill began to write plays in 1913. The following year he attended Dr. George Barker's playwriting course at Harvard. He subsequently moved to Greenwich Village, resuming the life of an alcoholic and derelict, supported by a dole from his father. In 1916 he moved to Provincetown, Massachusetts, and over the next two years a dozen of his short plays were produced by the Provincetown Players. His breakthrough came in 1920 when the full length play, *Beyond the Horizon*, was produced on Broadway.

O'Neill was a master of tragedy, observing that "The tragedy of life is what makes it worthwhile." He won the Pulitzer Prize three times, and in 1936 received the Nobel Prize for Literature. He died in 1953. His last words are said to have been, "Born in a hotel room—and God damn it—died in a hotel room!" The autobiographical play, *A Long Day's Journey into Night*, generally considered his masterpiece, was not published until two years after his death.

Nobel Prize winners are not immune from personal tragedy. Rudyard Kipling (Literature, 1907), the first Englishman to win the Nobel Prize for Literature, was one who suffered more than his share of bereavements.

Kipling was born in India in 1865, the son of a teacher of art. His first years were happy, until he was sent to school in England at the age of six. There, severe mistreatment by his foster-family almost broke his spirit. He went on to the United Services College, an institution mainly preparing young men for the armed services. This suited him better, although his book *Stalky and Co.* (1899), based on his experiences there, was described by Edmund Wilson as "a hair-raising picture of the sadism of the English public-school system." Kipling returned to India in 1882 and entered journalism, writing for and editing Anglo-Indian newspapers. He also began to write stories and poetry. *Plain Tales from the Hills* (1888) and *Barrack Room Ballads* (1892) made his name, and his fame spread with *The Jungle Book* in 1894. While he supported the ethos of the British Empire, Kipling was not uncritical of westernization:

"Asia is not going to be civilized after the methods of the West. There is too much Asia and she is too old."

Kipling returned to England in 1889. In 1892 he married Caroline Balestier, and they had two daughters and a son. After various travels, the Kiplings settled near Brattleboro in Vermont, where they were probably happiest. A quarrel with Kipling's brother-in-law ended this idyll, and the Kiplings returned to England. On a visit to New York in 1899, their much-loved daughter Josephine died of pneumonia. "Be thankful that you have never had a child to lose," he wrote to a friend. "I thought I knew something of what grief meant till that came to me." Throughout this period, and up to his death in 1936, Kipling continued to produce prodigious amounts of fiction and poetry. His sympathetic characters, often ordinary British soldiers, and his unerring ear for meter, made his stories and poetry wildly popular. In 1907, he was awarded the Nobel Prize for Literature. Kipling refused almost all other honors offered him, including the Poet Laureateship of England.

With the outbreak of war in 1914, Kipling, always an admirer of the military virtues, used his influence to obtain a commission for his son John in the Irish Guards, although the boy had been rejected by both the navy and the army on account of his severe myopia. John was killed in France at the Battle of Loos in 1915. Despite lengthy efforts, the boy's body was never discovered during Kipling's lifetime.

'Have you news of my boy Jack?'
Not this tide.
'When d'you think that he'll come back?'
Not with this wind blowing, and this tide.
'Has any one else had word of him?'
Not this tide.
For what is sunk will hardly swim,
Not with this wind blowing, and this tide.
'Oh, dear, what comfort can I find?'
None this tide,
Nor any tide,
Except he did not shame his kind
Not even with that wind blowing, and that tide.
Then hold your head up all the more,
This tide

And every
Because he was the son you bore,
And gave to that wind blowing and that tide!

What may we conclude from the lives of these laureates? Each of them suffered dearly the pains of defeat or bereavement. But in each case they succeeded in overcoming their grief and even turning it to good account. Jimmy Carter won the Nobel Prize for the work that he embarked on after his electoral defeat, and Winston Churchill won it largely due to his history of the war that he wrote while in opposition. Rudyard Kipling transmuted his bereavements into his poetry and short stories. It is not simply the experience of tragedy, but the way in which tragedy is confronted, that gives people greatness.

Another example is Kenzaburo Oe, the literature laureate of 1994. Kenzaburo Oe's son was born with severe brain damage, a heart-breaking challenge that Oe faced with great courage and determination.

Oe was born in 1935, on the island of Shikoku in Japan. From infancy he was exposed to stories told by his grandmother and other women of the Oe clan. His father died on active service during the war. His mother bought him books, such as *Huckleberry Finn*, that made a permanent impression on him.

Under the American administration following the war, democratic principles were taught in the schools, inspiring Oe to leave his native village and move to Tokyo, where he enrolled in the Department of French Literature at the University, writing his dissertation on Jean-Paul Sartre. He began to write and publish in 1957, while still a student. His early works depicted the dislocation and disorientation caused by Japan's surrender in 1945. At this stage he was dealing with the personal handicaps of shyness, a stutter, and a strong Shikoku accent.

His first son, Hikari, was born in 1963, with a cranial deformity that rendered him mentally handicapped. Oe rejected the doctors' advice to let the baby die. He wrote *A Personal Matter* (1964), recording his pain and his resolve to live with and care for his son. In his later fiction, he treats of the relationship between disabled and normal people. Hikari developed remarkable musical ability, becoming one of the best-known composers in Japan. "My son is named Hikari, which means 'light.' At his birth, even in my affliction, I named him 'Hikari.' Always, in darkness, I seek the light. "

In 1965, Oe published *Hiroshima Notes*, describing the effects of the nuclear bombing of Hiroshima and Nagasaki. In the 1960s, Oe joined the New Left movement, becoming a spokesman for radical causes especially opposition to nuclear weapons.

Oe received the Nobel Prize for Literature in 1994, for his works in which "poetic force creates an imagined world where life and myth condense to form a disconcerting picture of the human predicament today." He told an anecdote about receiving the prize.

> As a child, I wanted to be a physicist. I begged my mother to let me go to Tokyo to study physics. I promised I would win the Nobel Prize for Physics. So, 50 years later, I returned to my village and said to my mother, 'See, I have kept my promise. I won the Nobel Prize.' 'No,' said my mother, who has a very fine sense of humor, 'You promised it would be in physics!'

A Nobel laureate who suffered tragedy after winning the prize is Eric Cornell. He shared the prize for physics in 1961 with two other scientists for their work on Bose-Einstein condensation. In 2004 he was afflicted with necrotizing fasciitis, and had his left arm and shoulder amputated. On recovery, he agreed to a single press conference to discuss the event, at which he said, "Losing an arm is more an inconvenience than a catastrophe."

Chapter 18
I Belong to the
Russian Convict World

Hardship is neither a necessary nor a sufficient explanation of genius or success. However, many Nobel laureates experienced significant hardship en route to the Prize. One type of hardship is prison.

"I can say without affectation," wrote Aleksandr Solzhenitsyn, "that I belong to the Russian convict world no less... than I do to Russian literature. I got my education there, and it will last forever."

Prison has been a staging post for several laureates on their way to the Nobel Prize, but few were marked by the experience as deeply as Solzhenitsyn. He was born in Kislovodsk in the Caucasus Mountains in the Soviet Union in December 1918, six months after his father, who had served as an artillery officer through the First World War, was killed in a hunting accident. He was brought up by his mother, who worked as a shorthand-typist, in Rostov on the Don. Lacking the resources to go to Moscow to study literature, as he would have wished, he studied mathematics and physics at Rostov University, graduating shortly before the Nazi attack on the USSR. He served in the front lines for more than two years commanding an artillery-position-finding company. In February 1945 he was arrested on a charge of "anti-Soviet propaganda" on account of some disrespectful remarks about Stalin that he had made in a letter to a school friend. He was taken to the Lubyanka prison in Moscow where he was interrogated and beaten. He was sentenced to eight years detention.

Part of his sentence was served in a labor camp, under conditions which are described in *One Day in the Life of Ivan Denisovich*. The crowded sleeping quarters, the rising in the freezing dawn, the hurried and meager meals, the backbreaking work all day, the indifferent or brutal guards, the searches, the dangers from other convicts. But it was here also he learned significant lessons. One had to do with empathy: "Can a man, who is warm, understand one who's freezing?" Another concerned good and evil:

It was only when I lay there on rotting prison straw that I sensed within myself the first stirring of the good. Gradually it was disclosed to me that the line separating good and evil passes, not through states, not between classes, not between political parties either, but right through every human heart and through all human hearts.

His reminiscences are not without humor:

At the Novosibirsk Transit Prison in 1945 they greeted the prisoners with a roll call based on cases. "So and so! Article 51 and 58-1A, twenty-five years." The chief of the convoy guard was curious. 'What did you get it for?' 'For nothing at all.' 'You are lying. The sentence for nothing at all is ten years.'

Solzhenitsyn's background in mathematics and physics probably saved his life when, after four years, he was transferred from labor camp to a scientific research center operated by the Ministry of State Security. In 1950 he was sent to a camp for political prisoners in Kazakhstan where he worked as a miner, bricklayer, and foundry man. At the end of his sentence, he was sentenced to be exiled for life to a remote town in southern Kazakhstan, where he remained for three years, teaching mathematics and physics in a primary school. During this time, the stomach cancer that had developed in prison became critical, but he was treated and cured at a clinic in Tashkent.

He wrote in secret, believing that his work would never see publication. But after Khrushchev's "secret speech" to the 22nd Congress of the USSR, in 1956, which condemned the "cult of personality" and signaled the beginning of a thaw in political control, he submitted his novella, *One Day in the Life of Ivan Denisovich* to the publisher A.T. Tvardovsky, who published it in the magazine *Novy Mir*, with the explicit approval of Khrushchev. Three more of his novellas were published in 1963. Solzhenitsyn found himself famous, but the thaw did not last. Nothing more of his work was published in the Soviet Union for almost three decades. He was unable to get his books approved by the Union of writers, which expelled him, and his manuscripts were seized by the KGB.

Unable to publish at home, he had his work smuggled abroad for publication. His books *The First Circle and Cancer Ward* appeared in

1968-69. When his Nobel Prize was announced in 1970, the Soviet authorities denounced the award. Solzhenitsyn declined to go to Sweden to accept the Award, for fear that he would not be allowed to return home. After the first volume of *The Gulag Archipelago*, his monumental work on the prison camps in the Soviet Union, was published in the west in 1974, Solzhenitsyn was arrested and charged with treason. Stripped of his Soviet citizenship and exiled from the Soviet Union, he went to Switzerland and from there to the United States, where he lived for almost twenty years in Cavendish, Vermont. After the collapse of the USSR, he moved back to Russia in 1994, and settled in Moscow, where he died in 2008.

In his essay, "Live not by the lie," Solzhenitsyn wrote, "Let your creed be—Let the lie come into the world, let it even triumph—but not through me."

In another part of the Soviet empire, another future Nobel laureate suffered imprisonment a few years before Solzhenitsyn. Menachem Begin (Peace, 1978) was born in Brest-Litovsk, Poland, in 1913, and graduated in law from Warsaw University. In 1929 he became leader of Betar, the youth movement of the Zionist Revisionist leader Vladimir Jobotinsky. He was sent to Czechoslovakia to head the movement there.

In 1937 he returned to Poland, and for a time was imprisoned for leading a demonstration in front of the British Legation in Warsaw, protesting against British policy in Palestine. He organized groups of Betar members who went to Palestine as illegal immigrants, and in 1939 became the head of the movement in Poland. On the outbreak of World War II, he was arrested in Lithuania by the Russian authorities. He underwent many nights of interrogation in Lukishki Prison in Vilna before being sentenced to eight years in labor camp. The privations of this period strengthened his faith:

> It is a fact—and I saw it with my own eyes—that man in his downfall has nothing to lean on, nothing to solace him, except faith. The NKVD brought many back to the religious fold... Lukishki nights taught us that faith takes better care of man, when things go badly with him, than man does of his faith when things are well with him.

Then followed the seemingly endless train journey to Siberia, the thirsty and starving prisoners crowded into freight cars until they arrived at the correctional labour camp on the shore of the Barends Sea, where in winter the temperature dropped to 70 degrees below zero. Conditions were primitive, heavy labour was required for 12 hours a day, food was scarce, and lice, bedbugs, and voracious flies made life additionally miserable.

As a result of the German attack on Russia in 1941, an agreement was made between Russia and Poland, whereby Russia agreed to release all its Polish prisoners. Begin was already on a freighter carrying him further north when orders came for his release.

For the next several months, Begin walked south through Russia, looking for the Polish army which was, according to the Stalin-Sikorski agreement, to be formed on Russian soil. Eventually he found it, joined up, and was posted to Transjordan. There he deserted to Palestine, and soon assumed command of Irgun, the national combatant organization. The group was responsible for various violent acts against British rule and Palestinian communities. Begin directed operations against the British, and the Palestine Government offered a reward of £10,000 for information leading to his arrest, but he evaded capture by living in disguise in Tel Aviv. Irgun was disbanded in 1948, but only after an armed confrontation with the Israeli army.

After the establishment of the State of Israel, Begin founded the Herut or Freedom Party in 1948, becoming a member of the Knesset in 1949. In 1952 he led the opposition against the reparations agreement with West Germany. In 1973 he joined with other parties to form the Likud, which became the largest party in the election of May 1977. In 1977 he became Prime Minister of Israel. In 1978, President Carter organized meetings at Camp David between Menachem Begin and Anwar Al-Sadat, President of Egypt, which resulted in a frame agreement for concluding peace between Egypt and Israel. At the signing of the peace treaty the following year, Begin said: "No more war. No more bloodshed. No more bereavement. Peace unto you. Shalom, salaam, forever."

Menachem Begin and Anwar Al-Sadat shared the Nobel Prize for Peace in 1978. Anwar Al-Sadat, the President of Egypt, had also suffered imprisonment in his earlier days for his struggle against British rule in Egypt. He was assassinated in 1981 by Moslem extremists. Begin died in 1992.

It was in an earlier war that Bertrand Russell (Literature, 1950), the British philosopher, experienced prison. Russell was the grandson of Lord John Russell, who had been a prime minister under Queen Victoria. Deeply opposed to British involvement in the First World War, he was charged with sedition for a pamphlet he had written that cast aspersions on the American army. He had previously been convicted, but not imprisoned, for sedition in 1916, which had cost him his lectureship at Trinity College, Cambridge. In 1918 he was sentenced to six months in prison, of which he served four and a half months. The influence of friends saved him from being incarcerated in the most severe type of prison, where conscientious objectors were brutally treated, and had him committed to an institution where he was allowed reading and writing materials. He recollects arriving at the prison:

> I was much cheered on my arrival by the warder at the gate, who had to take particulars about me. He asked my religion, and I replied 'agnostic.' He asked how to spell it, and remarked with a sigh: 'Well, there are many religions, but I suppose they all worship the same God.' This remark kept me cheerful for about a week.

He took advantage of his prison time to write his <u>Introduction to Mathematical Philosophy</u> (1919). It was one of numerous books that earned him the Nobel Prize for Literature in 1950. That was not, however, the last time that Russell was to see the inside of prison walls. In 1961, at the age of 89, he took part in a sit-in protest in London against nuclear armament and was arrested. He was sentenced to two months imprisonment, but on appeal this was reduced to one week, which he served in a prison hospital. He died in 1970.

It may be supposed that the Nobel committees are favourably disposed toward people who have served time. This may be the case, but what is more certain is that they tend to select for the Nobel Prize individuals who have the courage of their convictions. Another such laureate is Wole Soyinka (Literature, 1986).

Soyinka was born in Western Nigeria in 1934, son of a primary school headmaster. At his secondary school he won several prizes for literary composition. He studied at Government College in Ibadan, and then at the University of Leeds in England. He spent six years in England, part of the time associated with the Royal Court Theatre in London. During this period he published many articles and wrote plays, two of which were performed in Ibadan. In 1960 he received a Rockefeller bursary and returned to Nigeria to study African drama. He taught at various universities in Nigeria, travelled widely through the country, and founded two theatre groups, in which he produced and acted in his own plays. His criticism of anti-democratic behavior by the authorities brought his arrest and imprisonment for several months.

During the civil war in Nigeria, Soyinka became involved in efforts to avert hostilities. He was accused of collaborating with Biafra and was imprisoned for 22 months, most of it in solitary confinement. While he was in prison, his plays continued to be performed in Nigeria and in New York. He reported an incident from his imprisonment in an interview in 1998:

> I was still under interrogation so I was in a cell and she was just thrown into that police cell with me. It was a holding room really. And at first she was very suspicious, she thought maybe I was just a spy, you know. And I think she just wasn't expecting to find anybody in that room, didn't know I'd just been under interrogation myself. So she was very withdrawn and very suspicious. And suddenly she looked down and saw that I was shackled, I was in chains. And so she slowly for the first time brought herself to actually look up and look at my face and recognize me. It was a very overwhelming and humbling moment because she then just took herself down at my feet and started to cry. It's reminiscent of one of those episodes of Christ, the woman washing his feet with her tears. In a way it was frightening. And then it became strengthening because I now had to console her, reassure her, and in turn I was strengthened. I became very, very strong both for her and for everybody in her situation.

Soyinka's protests against corruption and dictatorship in Nigeria have frequently put him in personal danger, and for long periods in exile. In 1997 the military regime in Nigeria sentenced him in absentia to death.

Soyinka has written numerous plays, two novels, a number of volumes of autobiography, and several volumes of poetry and of literary criticism. He was awarded the Nobel Prize for Literature in 1986. The presentation speech described him as a writer "who in a wide cultural perspective and with poetic overtones fashions the drama of existence."

On various occasions, the Nobel Prize has been used in the endeavour to extend protection to a fighter for peace or justice. The most pronounced case was that of Carl von Ossietzky, who died at the hands of the Nazis.

Ossietzky was born in Hamburg in 1889. His father died when Karl was two years old; when he was nine, his mother married Gustav Walther, a Social Democrat, whose political beliefs influenced those of Ossietzky. Carl left school at seventeen to enter the civil service, but soon turned to journalism. He was charged with "insult to the common good" for one of his anti-militarist articles, and was fined.

He was called up for military service in 1916, and his period in the army confirmed his pacifism:

> I know war as it is, not through reading about it... Supporters of peace have a duty and a task. It is to point out, over and over again, there is nothing heroic in war but that it brings terror and misery to mankind.

After the war he became president of the local chapter of the German Peace society, and then secretary of the national society. He next became foreign editor of the liberal *Berliner Volkszeitung*, and then joined the political weekly Tagebuch. In 1927 he became editor of *Die Weltbuhne*, a periodical that publicized Germany's secret rearmament. For one of the articles he published, Ossietzky was found guilty of libel and sentenced to one month in prison. In 1931 he was sentenced to eighteen months in jail for a similar publication, but was amnestied after seven months.

Despite his personal danger, Ossietzky refused to leave the country when the Nazis came to power. He was arrested the morning after the Reichstag fire in 1933, and sent to a concentration camp. Here he was badly abused and forced to perform heavy labor despite a bad heart. He was also suffering from tuberculosis.

An international campaign was launched by Ossietzky's supporters to gain him the Nobel Prize, and it was awarded to him in 1936. The Nazis refused to release him and demanded that he decline the prize, which Ossietzky refused to do. The German press was forbidden to mention the award of the prize to Ossietzky, and the government decreed that in future no German could accept a Nobel Prize. Ossietzky's lawyer embezzled the prize money. He was, however, transferred to a guarded hospital. He died there, as a result of his injuries from brutal treatment, in May 1938.

A woman of similar invincible courage was Wangari Maathai (Peace, 2004), who, in pursuit of her environmental ideals, endured imprisonment, beating, and death threats.

Maathai was born in a small village in Kenya in 1940, to a Kikuyu peasant family. She was educated at Catholic schools in Kenya, and then became part of the "Kennedy Airlift," a program sponsored by then senator John F. Kennedy to provide scholarships for African students to study in the United States. She received her B.A. in biology from Mount St. Scholastica College in Kansas, then went to the University of Pittsburgh for graduate study, earning her M.A. in biology in 1966. She writes of this period:

> It is fair to say that America transformed me. It made me into the person I am today... The spirit of freedom and possibility that America nurtured in me made me want to foster the same in Kenya, and it was in this spirit that I returned home.

After her return to Kenya, Wangari obtained a position in the Department of Veterinary Science at Makerere University, and registered for her Ph.D. Her doctoral studies took her to Germany, where she spent almost two years, adding German to her English, Kikuyu, and Kiswahili. She received her doctorate in 1971, becoming the first East African woman to earn a Ph.D. In 1969 she married Mwangi Mathai, with whom she had three children. Despite the experience of gender discrimination in the university, she became chair of the Department of Veterinary Anatomy in 1976.

Wangari became chair of the National Council of Women of Kenya, and was involved in numerous non-governmental organizations. She was co-chair of the Jubilee 2000 Africa Campaign, which sought cancellation of the unpayable backlog of debt owed by African countries to the West. She ran for parliament, was disqualified on a technicality, and in the process lost her university position. She started the Green Belt

Movement, an organization that engaged women in planting trees. Eventually the movement would establish more than six thousand nurseries, involve several hundred thousand women, and plant more than thirty million trees. The movement also spread to other African countries, including Tanzania, Uganda, Malawi, Ethiopia, and Zimbabwe.

Wangari's marriage ended in divorce in 1977. Her remarks on the bias shown by the judge earned her jail time for contempt of court. She next came into direct conflict with the government over plans to build a 60-storey office building in Uhuru Park in the center of Nairobi. Eventually the government abandoned the plan. The government of Daniel Arap Moi had become increasingly authoritarian, and Wangari became part of the pro-democracy movement. As a result she was arrested and jailed on a number of occasions, once beaten unconscious, subject to death threats, often forced to live in hiding, and constantly harassed by the police.

When democracy was restored in Kenya in the 2002 election, Wangari was elected a member of parliament with 98 per cent of the vote. She was appointed Assistant Minister in the Ministry for Environment, Natural Resources and Wildlife. In 2004 she received the Nobel Peace Prize.

> I have seen time and again that if you stay with a challenge, if you are convinced that you are right to do so, and if you give it everything you have, it is amazing what can happen.

Wangari Maathai died in 2011.

One of the best-known Nobel laureates is Aung San Suu Kyi (Peace, 1991), leader of the Burma Democracy Movement, who spent much of her adult life under house arrest in Burma (Myanmar).

Suu Kyi was born in 1945, daughter of Aung San, founder of the modern Burmese army, who negotiated Burma's independence from the United Kingdom in 1947, and was assassinated the same year. She grew up with her mother and brothers in Yangon. Suu Kyi was educated in English Catholic schools during her childhood. Her mother was appointed ambassador to India in 1960, and Suu Kyi accompanied her, graduating from Lady Shri Ram College in New Delhi in 1964. She continued her education at St. Hugh's College Oxford, earning a B.A.

degree in Philosophy, Politics, and Economics in 1969, and a Ph.D. from the School of Oriental and African Studies at the University of London in 1985. In 1969, she joined the UN secretariat in New York as an Assistant Secretary, and did volunteer work at a local hospital.

In 1972 she married Dr. Michael Aris, a scholar of Tibetan culture then living in Bhutan. She joined him in Bhutan, where he was a tutor to the royal family, returning to Britain for the birth of the first of their two sons. They lived in Oxford, where Michael had received an appointment in Tibetan and Himalayan studies. During this period, Suu Kyi wrote and published extensively on topics connected with Burma.

In 1988, Suu Kyi returned to Burma to care for her ailing mother. That year the leader of the socialist ruling party, General New Win, stepped down, leading to mass pro-democracy demonstrations, which were violently suppressed. Suu Kyi addressed a mass rally of half a million people, and called for a democratic government. A new military junta took power. Suu Kyi helped found the National League for Democracy in September 1988, and was put under house arrest the next year. She was offered freedom if she left the country, but she refused.

In 1990, the military junta called a general election, which the National League for Democracy won with 82 per cent of the vote. Instead of becoming Prime Minister, Suu Kyi was placed under house arrest, and the military refused to hand over power. She was warned that if she left the country she would not be allowed to return. When her husband was dying of cancer, the government refused him an entry visa, and she was unable to see him before his death. She also remained separated from her two sons, who live in Britain. For the most part of the next two decades, Suu Kyi remained under house arrest, from which she was released in 2010. In 2015, she led her party to a majority in the Myanmar parliament.

A woman of serene dignity and courage, Suu Kyi is fortified by her Buddhist faith. On one occasion, when soldiers aimed their rifles at the crowd at one of her rallies, she said, "We are grateful to those who are giving the people practice in being brave." It is her belief that the fundamental freedom is freedom from fear:

> It is not power that corrupts but fear. Fear of losing power corrupts those who wield it and fear of the scourge of power corrupts those who are subject to it.

Suu Kyi was awarded the Nobel Prize for Peace in 1991. Her sons Alexander and Kim accepted the award on her behalf. She used the prize money to establish a health and education trust for the Burmese people. That year, she wrote:

> Saints, it has been said, are the sinners who go on trying. So, free men and women are the oppressed who go on trying and who in the process make themselves fit to bear the responsibilities and uphold the disciplines which will maintain a free society.

Kim Dae-Jung (Peace, 2000) survived imprisonment, exile, and assassination attempts before becoming President of South Korea and being awarded the Nobel Peace Prize.

Kim Dae-Jung was born in 1925 on an island off the coast of South Korea. He attended a commercial high school, graduating in 1943. He entered politics in 1954 and in 1961 ran successfully for a seat in the National Assembly in a by-election, but three days later General Park Chung Hee overthrew the government in a military coup and dissolved the National Assembly. Kim was re-elected in 1963 and 1967, becoming a leader of the opposition. In 1971 he ran for president against General Park, losing by a slim margin. At this time he experienced the first of several assassination attempts; a heavy truck ran into his car, leaving him with serious wounds and a permanently injured leg.

When President Park imposed martial law, banning all political activity and proclaiming a new constitution that gave him power for life, Kim led the campaign against the regime. In his Nobel lecture, Kim described what happened next:

> I have lived, and continue to live, in the belief that God is always with me. I know this from experience. In August of 1973, while exiled in Japan, I was kidnapped from my hotel room in Tokyo by intelligence agents of the then military government of South Korea. The news of the incident startled the world. The agents took me to their boat at anchor along the seashore. They tied me up, blinded me, and stuffed my mouth. Just when they were about to throw me overboard, Jesus Christ appeared before me with such clarity. I clung to him and begged him to save me. At that very moment, an airplane came down from the sky to rescue me from the moment of death.

He was released after protests from the US and Japan, and placed under house arrest. In 1976 he was sentenced to five years in prison, converted to house arrest in 1978. A new military regime imprisoned him again in 1980 on a charge of treason. He was sentenced to death by a military court, later commuted to life imprisonment, then to 20 years. In 1982 he was allowed to leave Korea for the United States. He returned to Korea in 1985 and was put under house arrest. In 1987 he was cleared of all charges. He ran unsuccessfully for president in 1987 and 1992. In 1997 he was elected president of South Korea. He adopted a policy of engagement with North Korea, holding the first presidential summit with the North Korean leader, Kim Jong-il.

In 2000, Kim Dae-Jung was awarded the Nobel Peace Prize. In a 2001 interview, he expressed his philosophy of life:

> I have to say that I am not a strong person. I am not a courageous person. I do not have that much courage. But despite coming close to death five times, being in prison for six years, being in house arrest and exile overseas for over thirty years, it is my aspiration to live a right life by my standard. If that requires sacrifice and that requires pain, I have to do so.

Kim Dae-Jung died in 2009.

No Nobel laureate spent longer in prison Nelson Mandela (Peace, 1993), who spent 27 years in South African jails.

Nelson Mandela was born in Transkei, South Africa in 1918. His father was Chief Henry Mandela of the Tembu Tribe, and his grandfather was king of the Tembu people. Mandela was the son of the third of his father's four wives. He was the first of his family to attend school, where he was given the name Nelson. In secondary school he took an interest in running and boxing. He received his university education at University College of Fort Hare and the University of Witwatersrand and qualified in law in 1942. During this period he made many lifelong friends who became allies in the struggle against apartheid. He joined the African National Congress in 1944 and was engaged in resistance against the ruling National Party's apartheid policies after 1948. He went on trial with 150 others for treason in 1956-1961 but after a marathon trial all were acquitted in 1961.

After the banning of the ANC in 1960, Nelson Mandela argued for the setting up of a military wing within the ANC. In June 1961, the ANC executive considered his proposal on the use of violent tactics and agreed that those members who wished to involve themselves in Mandela's campaign would not be stopped from doing so by the ANC. This led to the formation of Umkhonto we Sizwe. Mandela coordinated bombing campaigns against military and government targets, making plans for a possible guerrilla war, and raising funds and organizing paramilitary training. Of his political development, Mandela later wrote in *Long Walk to Freedom*:

> I had no epiphany, no singular revelation, no moment of truth, but a steady accumulation of a thousand slights, a thousand indignities, a thousand unremembered moments, produced in me an anger, a rebelliousness, a desire to fight the system that imprisoned my people.

Mandela was arrested in 1962 and sentenced to five years' imprisonment with hard labor. In 1963, when many fellow leaders of the ANC and the Umkhonto we Sizwe were arrested, Mandela was brought to stand trial with them for plotting to overthrow the government by violence. In his defense, Mandela argued that force was adopted as a last resort after all nonviolent means of protest against apartheid had failed. He said:

> During my lifetime I have dedicated my life to this struggle of the African people. I have fought against white domination, and I have fought against black domination. I have cherished the ideal of a democratic and free society in which all persons live together in harmony and with equal opportunities. It is an ideal which I hope to live for, and to achieve. But if needs be, it is an ideal for which I am prepared to die.

His statement from the dock received considerable international publicity. On June 12, 1964, eight of the accused, including Mandela, were sentenced to life imprisonment. From 1964 to 1982, he was incarcerated at Robben Island Prison, off Cape Town. He worked in the prison quarry, and was allowed one visitor and one letter every six months. In a letter to his wife Winnie Mandela, he wrote, "A saint is a sinner that keeps on trying." While in prison he studied for and received a Bachelor of Laws degree from the University of London. In 1982, Mandela was transferred to Pollsmoor Prison, on the mainland.

During his years in prison, Nelson Mandela's reputation grew steadily. He was widely accepted as the most significant black leader in South Africa and became a potent symbol of resistance as the anti-apartheid movement gathered strength. During his imprisonment, Mandela began to work on his autobiography, eventually published as *Long Walk to Freedom*. In 1985 the government offered Mandela freedom in exchange for his renouncing armed struggle; he refused. In 1990, President F. W. de Klerk reversed the ban on the ANC and announced the release of Nelson Mandela.

Nelson Mandela was released on February 11, 1990. After his release, he plunged himself wholeheartedly into his life's work, striving to attain the goals he and others had set out almost four decades earlier. In 1991, at the first national conference of the ANC held inside South Africa after the organization had been banned in 1960, Mandela was elected President of the ANC.

In 1993, Nelson Mandela and Frederick de Klerk shared the Nobel Peace Prize. In the 1994 election, the ANC won 62 per cent of the Votes, and Mandela became President of South Africa. In his inaugural address, he said:

> The time for the healing of the wounds has come. The moment to bridge the chasms that divide us has come. The time to build is upon us... Let there be justice for all. Let there be peace for all. Let there be work, bread, water and salt for all.

So far, we have looked at Nobel laureates who were imprisoned for their political convictions. But they are not the only laureates to have suffered imprisonment. Several were interned as military or civilian prisoners of war. Both the German writers, Günter Grass (Literature, 1999) and Heinrich Böll (Literature, 1972) were captured by the Americans at the end of the war and spent time in POW camps. Jean-Paul Sartre, as a soldier in the French army, was captured by the Germans in 1941, but escaped. Manfred Eigen was captured by Russians on the Eastern Front at the age of 17. He escaped from prison camp, walked across half of Europe back to Germany, and immediately enrolled at Gottingen University, despite having no high school diploma. He got his doctorate there, and in 1967 won the Nobel Prize for Chemistry. James Chadwick

(Physics 1935) was studying in Berlin when World War I broke out. He was imprisoned in a horse stable for the duration of the war, where he was nevertheless allowed to set up a laboratory.

The ethologist, Konrad Lorenz, was captured by the Russians, and not released until 1947. As a doctor, he was allowed to practice his profession while in captivity, working in hospitals and camps in Armenia. He wrote:

> In spring 1942 I was sent to the front near Witebsk and two months later taken prisoner by the Russians.... I became tolerably fluent in Russian and got quite friendly with some Russians, mostly doctors. I had the occasion to observe the striking parallels between the psychological effects of Nazi and of Marxist education. It was then that I began to realize the nature of indoctrination as such.

In his spare time he wrote a book on epistemology, using potassium permanganate solution as ink, and pieces of cement sacking for paper.

At the end of the war, there was a race between the Russians and the West to capture German scientists. Ten German physicists were captured by the British and taken to a guarded country house, Farm Hall, in England. The group included three Nobel laureates: Werner Heisenberg (Physics 1932), Max von Laue (Physics1914), and Otto Hahn (Chemistry 1944). The British were most interested to know how far the Germans had proceeded in their efforts to build an atomic bomb. Unknown to the scientists, their conversations at Farm Hall were recorded. When they heard the news of the atomic bomb exploded at Hiroshima, their conversation shows how impressed they were by the allied achievement, and how glad they were that they had not succeeded to the same extent. Otto Hahn was deeply upset by the news. He had first split the atom, and he felt a burden of responsibility for the carnage that the atom bomb had produced. He exclaimed, "I thank God on bended knees that we did not make the uranium bomb."

What may we deduce from these accounts? First, perhaps, is corroboration of Nietzsche's remark that "What does not kill me, makes me stronger." Prison killed Ossietzky, as it killed millions in Germany, the Soviet Union, and elsewhere in the world. But the other future laureates emerged from prison with their lives intact and their convictions strengthened. From the point of view of the authorities, the punishment was counter-productive. Jawaharlal Nehru, later prime minister of India, was imprisoned by the British under fairly relaxed conditions for his advocacy of Indian independence. He found he was able to write without interruption: "All my major works have been written in prison. I would recommend prison not only to aspiring writers but to aspiring politicians too."

Solzhenitsyn goes further. In his autobiographical novel, *The First Circle*, he follows the life story of the mathematician Gleb Nerzhin, a convict working in a scientific establishment.

> In every human being's life there is one period when he manifests himself most fully, feels most profoundly himself, and acts with the deepest effect on himself and on others. And whatever happens to that person from that time on, no matter how outwardly significant, it is all a letdown. We remember, get drunk on, play over and over in many different keys, sing over and over to ourselves that snatch of a song that sounded just once within us. ...For Nerzhin, prison was such a time.

Chapter 19
A Century of Exile

For many laureates who avoided prison, exile was the price of their ultimate success, and often of their immediate survival.

Everyone understands exile. As babies, we are exiles from the womb; as adults, we are exiles from childhood. Those are fortunate who do not, at some point in their life, find themselves exiles from a once-cherished relationship.

For millions of people, the 20th century was a century of exile. So it was for Nobel Prize winners. We have already noted how the passage of the Nazi racial laws in Germany, and similar legislation in Austria and Italy led to the emigration of scientists to Britain and the United States. Baruch Shalev estimates that 47 American Nobel laureates were Jews who fled anti-Semitism in Europe.

In addition to the Jewish scientists who escaped from Nazi-controlled Europe, there were others displaced by war or who were voluntarily or involuntarily exiled from Eastern Europe. One such was Joseph Brodsky.. He was born in Leningrad in 1940, the son of a photographer. At the age of 14, he applied for admission to a submarine academy, but was rejected on account of being Jewish. He dropped out of school at 15, and worked at many different jobs, including as a machine operator, a stoker, work in a morgue and boiler room, and as a member of geological expeditions. He began writing poetry when he was 18. His poetry was too unorthodox to be published in official journals; consequently it appeared in samizdat publications. He also became an important translator from English and Polish into Russian.

In 1963, Brodsky was arrested on a charge that he was a "tuneyadets" or social parasite. Following is an excerpt from his trial:

Judge: In general, what is your specialty?
Brodsky: Poet. Poet and translator.
Judge: And who decided that you are a poet? Who put you in the ranks of the poets?
Brodsky: Nobody. And who put me in the ranks of mankind?
Judge: Did you study for this?

Brodsky: Study for what?

Judge: To become a poet. You never tried to finish college where they prepare, where they study…

Brodsky: I didn't think that this was a matter of education.

Judge: And if not through education, how is it?

Brodsky: I thought, well, I thought it came from God.

Brodsky was sentenced to five years hard labor. Witnesses who had spoken up on his behalf were persecuted by the KGB. Brodsky now entered the world of the Gulag Archipelago. Twice he was sent to psychiatric hospitals:

> They gave me terrible shots… Woke me up in the middle of the night, forced me to take baths in ice-cold water, then would wrap me up in a wet sheet and put me down next to the radiator. The heat dried the sheet and tore the skin off my body.

He served time in three prisons, including the notorious Leningrad prison, the Crosses, where beatings were more or less routine. He observed that "The formula for prison is a lack of space counterbalanced by a surplus of time." Finally he ended up exiled to the Arkhangelsk region of Siberia near the Arctic Circle, in a village of 14 people, where he did heavy agricultural labor. After protests from internationally known individuals, including the composer Dmitri Shostakovich, the philosopher Jean-Paul Sartre, and the poet Anna Akhmatova, the term was reduced, and he was released after 18 months.

Two of Brodsky's books were published abroad. In 1972 he was forced into exile from the Soviet Union. He was separated from his four-year-old son, and never saw his parents again. He went first to Vienna, whence the poet W. H. Auden helped him to emigrate to the United States. He made his home in New York, and taught as a visiting professor at several universities. His many volumes of poetry and essays were widely praised and translated. He once remarked, "I'm the happiest combination you can think of. I'm a Russian poet, an English essayist, and an American citizen!" In 1987, he was awarded the Nobel Prize for Literature. He died of a heart attack in 1996.

Despite the hardships of his life, Brodsky refused to become embittered. In a commencement address at the University of Michigan, he said"

At all costs try to avoid granting yourself the status of the victim… No matter how abominable your condition may be, try not to blame anything or anybody.

"My blood runs cold," wrote Czeslaw Milosz, "when I pronounce the words: the twentieth century." For him, like Brodsky, exile became the primary disjuncture of his life. Of this he was fully conscious. In an interview in 1987, he said, "In the twentieth century exile seems almost to be the universal condition of the writer." And in an article entitled "Notes on Exile," he wrote, "To express the existential situation of modern man, one must live in exile of some sort." In his Nobel acceptance speech, he said:

> Since I have lived a long time in exile, I may be legitimately claimed by all those who had to leave their native villages and provinces because of misery or persecution and to adapt themselves to new ways of life; we are millions all over the Earth, for this is a century of exile.

Milosz was born in Lithuania in 1911, the son of a civil engineer. He completed high school and university in Wilno, at that time in Poland. He published two volumes of poetry in 1933. During World War II, he worked for underground presses in Warsaw. He entered the Polish diplomatic service in 1945, and served until 1951, when he defected to France. He wrote several prose works there, receiving the Prix Littéraire Européen in 1953. In 1960, he was invited to the University of California at Berkeley, where he stayed for twenty years. After winning the Nobel Prize in 1980, his work, hitherto banned, began to be published in Poland, and from the mid-1980s he divided his time between Cracow and Berkeley. He died in Cracow in 2003, at the age of 93.

A particular case of exile occurred in the case of Peter Kapitsa, the Russian physicist. Peter Kapitsa was a brilliant Russian scientist, working in Cambridge, when his career was brutally interrupted by being detained in the Soviet Union.

Kapitsa was born in Kronstadt, near Leningrad, in 1894. His father was a lieutenant-general in the Corps of Engineers, and his mother a teacher. He graduated in 1918 from the Electromechanics Department of the Petrograd Polytechnical Institute. His wife and children died during the chaos of the Civil War following the Revolution. In 1921 he applied for a visa to work in Britain; it was obtained through the intercession of the writer Maxim Gorky. He went to the Cavendish Laboratory in Cambridge to work with Ernest Rutherford, with whom he formed a warm friendship. He soon established himself as an outstanding physicist, working in cloud chamber and low temperature research. He was awarded his doctorate in 1923, and the same year won the James Clark Maxwell Prize. He became Assistant Director of Magnetic Research at the Cavendish Laboratory and Director of the Mond Laboratory. He was one of the very few foreigners to be elected to the Royal Society. In 1927 he married Anna Alekseevna Krylova, daughter of Academician A.N. Krylov. Kapitsa was a man of wide interest and sympathies; on one occasion he commented, "Ah, but it is impossible to live without poetry!"

On a visit to Russia in 1934, Kapitsa was refused permission to leave on Stalin's orders. Appeals by himself and by Rutherford in England had no effect. Exiled from his adoptive home, deprived of his laboratory, his equipment, and his scientific colleagues, the enforced idleness almost drove him to despair. He had always believed that "The moment even the greatest scientist stops his own work in the laboratory, he not only ceases his growth, but is no longer a scientist." Eventually he organized the Institute for Physical Problems of which he became director, and his equipment was shipped to Russia from Cambridge, purchased by the Soviets for £30,000. He was thus able to continue his research on magnetic fields and low temperature physics. For his work on hyperfluidity, Kapitsa received the Stalin Prize in 1941 and 1943, and he was made a hero of Socialist Labor in 1945 for his research into turbine methods of oxygen production. He also received the Soviet Union's highest honor, the Order of Lenin.

During the war, he worked on large-scale production of oxygen for the steel industry, but was later disgraced for refusing to work on nuclear weapons. Probably he was under house arrest during Stalin's later years. Despite his refusal to join the Communist Party, he became a member of the Presidium of the USSR Academy of Sciences. He campaigned to save Lake Baikal and was a member of the Pugwash movement for peaceful use of science. When the physicist Lev Landau (Physics 1962) was arrested, he intervened directly with Stalin to secure his release, probably thereby saving his life. He also petitioned Brezhnev on behalf of Andrei Sakharov.

Kapitsa campaigned for greater freedom for Soviet scientists to choose their area of work and to travel abroad. He himself was eventually allowed to travel, to Denmark in 1965 and to Britain in 1966. Kapitsa was awarded the Nobel Prize for Physics in 1978, for his work in low-temperature physics. He died in 1984.

Gao Xingjian (Literature, 2000), the Chinese writer, experienced double exile, first within his own country, and then by leaving it.

Xingjian was born in Jiangxi province in Eastern China in 1940. His father was a bank official and his mother an amateur actress and avid reader of western literature. As a child, with parental encouragement, he wrote, painted, and played the violin. In 1962 he graduated from Beijing Foreign Studies University with a degree in French and literature. In the early 1960s, Xingjian's mother, who had been sent to work in the countryside, drowned in an accident. During the Cultural Revolution, on account of his background, he was sent for several years to a re-education camp for "reform through labor" where gruelling work was interrupted only by public recitations of the thoughts of Chairman Mao. In his autobiographical novel, *One Man's Bible*, he describes this as "intensive physical labour designed to snuff out thinking and to punish anyone with an education or capable of reflective thinking." To avoid being compromised, he burned a suitcase full of manuscripts. He later moved to a village in the mountains.

When he was allowed to return to Beijing, he worked as a translator in the Chinese Writers Association, and became resident playwright at the People's Art Theatre. In 1978 he published his first novella. In 1979 he had the opportunity to travel abroad, and visited France and Italy. In the 1980s he published four books and numerous essays, short stories, and dramas. His works were politically controversial; his play *Bus Stop* (1983) was described by a Communist Party official as "the most pernicious work since the establishment of the People's Republic." In 1986, he was wrongly diagnosed with lung cancer, the disease that had killed his father. He undertook a ten-month walking tour tracing the route of the Yangzi River from its source to the coast. This journey eventually produced his celebrated novel, *Soul Mountain* (1989).

In 1986 his play, *The Other Shore*, was banned. The following year Xingjian, although now a blacklisted writer, was allowed to leave China as a painter, and he sought refugee status in France. His works were subsequently banned by the Chinese government. He became a French citizen in 1997:

> I'm not involved in politics, but that does not prevent me from criticizing the policies of Communist China. I say what I want to say. If I have chosen to live in exile, it is to be able to express myself freely without constraints.

Xingjian paints in ink and has held many international exhibitions of his graphic work. He has also translated into Chinese works by Beckett, Ioneso, Artaud, and Brecht. In 2000, he was awarded the Nobel Prize for Literature, "for an oeuvre of universal validity, bitter insights and linguistic ingenuity, which has opened new paths for the Chinese novel and drama". Xingjian has written his own statement of the significance of the writer:

> Literature is a place of refuge for the free spirit and the last bastion of defence for human dignity. Herein lies the gift of the writer: when people have turned mute because of their sufferings, God blesses him with a voice.

Herta Müller, who won the Nobel Prize for literature in 2009, is another exile, in her case from Romania to Germany. In Ceausescu's Romania, she was constantly under surveillance, her apartment frequently searched, and she herself often interrogated. She refused to cooperate with the Securitate; in return, they put about the rumour that she was spying for them. On one occasion she was taken in for interrogation, and she describes an exchange with a Securitate officer:

> He said I was having sex with eight Arab students in exchange for tights and cosmetics. I didn't know a single Arab student. When I told him this, he replied: "If we want to, we'll find 20 Arabs as witnesses. You'll see, it'll make for a splendid trial."

Her friends and readers were put under surveillance, a German journalist attempting to interview her was brutally beaten, and one of her friends was found hanged in his flat; this was immediately declared a suicide. In 1987, Müller emigrated to Germany, but the surveillance by the

Securitate continued. Nor did the smear campaign cease with the fall of Ceausescu in 1989.

Whether their exile is forced or voluntary, Nobel laureates tend to go to the place where they can work most effectively. Albert Einstein was born in Switzerland, and did his Nobel-winning work there; he also worked in Germany. Later, when the Nazis came to power, Einstein vowed never to return to Germany. After some months of wandering, he arrived at the Institute for Advanced Research at Princeton, where he spent the rest of his career. T. S. Eliot (Literature 1948) crossed the Atlantic in the other direction. Born in St. Louis, Missouri in 1888, and educated at Harvard, he went to Britain to study at Oxford, and found it a country that was congenial to his way of life and thought. He stayed there until he died in 1965.

Baruch Shalev analyzed "brain migration" among Nobel laureates. He found a general movement from less developed to more developed countries and from more oppressive to less oppressive states. 23% of chemistry laureates credited their Nobel to a different country than that of their birth. The figure was 32% in Medicine, 20% in physics, 26% in economics, 18% in Literature, and 10% in peace. About one third of these cases were Jewish individuals escaping from Nazi Germany and Austria. The statistics also include nine laureates who moved from Canada to the United States.

The pattern that is apparent is similar to the migration of leading scholars toward elite universities: future Nobel laureates leave countries that cannot or will not support their work and go to countries where their work will be best supported. In so doing they reveal a resilience that enables them to overcome the dislocation that accompanies exile from their homeland.

Chapter 20
An Era of War

We have already noted that courage often accompanies success. This is particularly marked in times of war. War loomed large in the experience of many twentieth-century Nobel laureates. Many of them served in their countries' armed forces, often with distinction. Others engaged in war work as civilians. During the Second World War, several Nobel laureates participated in the Resistance against the Nazi occupation in Europe. This roll of honor includes André Lwoff, Jacques Monod, Albert Camus, Jean-Paul Sartre, Georges Pire, Albert Szent-Gyorgyi, Georges Charpak (Physics, 1992), Frédéric Joliot-Curie (Chemistry, 1935), Czeslaw Milosz, Renato Dulbecco, Willy Brandt, and Samuel Beckett.

Albert Szent-Gyorgyi (he asked his English-speaking friends to pronounce his name Saint Georgie) was deeply affected by both World Wars. He was born in Hungary in 1893, the son of a wealthy landowner. His uncle was a famous physiologist, but, like Albert's father, had doubts about his ability. Nevertheless, Albert entered medical school. His studies were interrupted by the outbreak of World War I. As a student, Albert was already enrolled in the army, and was sent to the eastern front, where he received the silver medal for valor for rescuing wounded soldiers under fire. In 1916, disgusted by the war, he shot himself in the arm, using his anatomical knowledge to ensure the wound would not be permanently disabling. He returned to medical school, but his real interest was always in basic research.

During the 1920s and 1930s, Albert lived the life of a wandering scientist, often poverty-stricken, working at several different universities, including five years at Cambridge. In the 1930s he isolated Vitamin C, for which he was awarded the Nobel Prize in 1937. He dealt with the $40,000 prize money in a unique way:

> I knew World War II was coming and I was afraid that if I had shares which rise in case of war, I would wish for war. So I asked my broker to buy shares which go down in the event of war. This he did. I lost my money but saved my soul.

The dictator of Hungary was Admiral Horthy, who was pro-fascist and anti-Semitic. Albert, by now Director of the medical chemical laboratory at Szeged, did what he could for persecuted Jewish students and professors, finding jobs abroad for Jewish colleagues who were dismissed from their posts. When war broke out, Horthy's government declared war on the side of the Nazis.

In 1942, Albert joined other intellectuals in founding the Hungarian Front of National Independence. In the following year he formed the Citizens Democratic Party. He travelled secretly to Istanbul to open negotiations with the Allies in the name of the Hungarian opposition. This became known to Hitler, who, at his next meeting with Horthy, screamed that he wanted Szent-Gyorgyi arrested and sent to Germany. Albert went underground and spent the rest of the war in hiding, several times narrowly escaping capture. In the winter of 1944-45, as the Russians began to encircle Budapest, Albert was invited to a secret meeting of the Resistance at a restaurant. His biographer relates the incident:

> Just as he reached the restaurant, where the meeting was to be held, he turned back. There was no particular reason to be afraid, but his intuition warned against it. And, indeed, the whole thing was a trap... the café was packed with S.S. men, ready to pounce on him.

With the ending of the war, Albert was feted as a national hero, both in Hungary and the Soviet Union. But as the Communist grip on Hungary tightened in the post-war years, he found himself increasingly at odds with official policy. In 1947 he moved with his wife and daughter to the United States. He built a home at Woods Hole, Massachusetts, where he worked on muscle metabolism with the aid of grants from the Rockefeller Foundation and the U.S. Navy. Eventually he became director of his own funding organization, the National Foundation for Cancer Research. During the 1960s and 1970s, he frequently spoke out against the Vietnam War and the threat of nuclear weapons. He never stopped working, making major breakthroughs in the study of muscle chemistry. He died in 1986, at the age of 93. Asked late in life for his credo, he said, "Think boldly. Don't be afraid of making mistakes. Don't miss small details, keep your eyes open and be modest in everything except your aims."

Another group of scientists directly affected by the Second World War were those recruited to work on the atomic bomb in the United States. A remote site at Los Alamos, New Mexico, was chosen to headquarter the Manhattan project. The wooden buildings there had previously housed a ranch school for boys. The site was chosen by the scientific director of the Manhattan Project, J. Robert Oppenheimer, together with General Leslie Groves and Physicist Ernest Lawrence (Physics 1939). Officially the place did not exist. It was known as "Site Y", but residents received their mail at "P. O. Box 1663, Santa Fe." Eventually about 6000 people lived at Los Alamos, in 300 apartment buildings, 52 dormitories, and 200 trailers. Hans Bethe (Physics 1967) reports a story about Lamy, which was the nearest railroad station to Los Alamos.

> There was a story about some people who went to the railroad station in Princeton to buy tickets to Lamy, and the ticket seller told them, "Don't go there. Twenty people have already gone there, and not one of them has ever come back."

Although isolated and surrounded by barbed wire, Los Alamos provided hiking, horse riding, skiing, and square dancing. Life was enlivened by such characters as Richard Feynman, one of whose hobbies was opening safes and locked filing cabinets. Other Nobel physicists who worked at Los Alamos included Enrico Fermi, Niels Bohr, Isidor Rabi, Hans Betheand James Chadwick. Joseph Rotblat (Peace, 1995) worked on the project until it was clear that Germany was beaten, and then resigned. Others employed on the Manhattan Project outside Los Alamos included Arthur Compton (Physics, 1927) and Edward Lawrence. The rationale of most scientists was that, in view of the number of gifted nuclear physicists still left in Germany, that country would be endeavouring to build a nuclear weapon, and the Allies must therefore achieve this first.

The Allies made every effort to discover how advanced nuclear physics was in Germany. Planes were sent over Germany trailing wicks into rivers to check for radioactivity. Werner Heisenberg's expertise was well known. When Heisenberg was to give a lecture in Switzerland, the Office of Strategic Services sent an agent to attend the lecture. The agent was the multilingual Moe Berg, who before the war had for fifteen years been a catcher in major league baseball. Berg's instructions were that if Heisenberg mentioned atomic research, Berg was to shoot him on the spot. But Heisenberg made no such reference; Berg's pistol remained in his pocket, and both he and Heisenberg survived the war. Heisenberg was in fact in charge of nuclear research in Nazi Germany, but his efforts did not go further than initial work on a reactor. Historians still debate whether or not this lack of progress was deliberate on Heisenberg's part.

A scientist who earned the Nobel Prize after his work at Los Alamos was Val Fitch (Physics 1980). He was born in 1923 in Nebraska, where his father was a cattle rancher, and was educated in local public schools. He interrupted his college science degree to join the army in 1941, and in 1942 was sent to Los Alamos to work on the Manhattan Project. As a member of a military unit known as the Special Engineer Detachment he worked in a technical capacity under a British physicist, Ernest Titterton. His group's main task concerned fast timing measurements of detonation phenomena. During his three years at Los Alamos, he came to know and respect many of the great men of physics employed on the project, including Enrico Fermi, Niels Bohr, James Chadwick, and Isidor Rabi, both in the workplace and on neighboring ski slopes:

> A number of young men like myself, very early in their lives and careers, were exposed to superb physicists who were remarkable people in many respects, and it had a profound influence upon us... At Los Alamos I learned that, by and large, physicists were extraordinary people. The complete intellectual integrity required in the pursuit of physics carried over into the personal relationships of physicists.

Although security prevented SED members from becoming officers, and enforced a life of considerable isolation at Los Alamos, most enlisted men found the work intellectually stimulating. Fitch was present at the first nuclear explosion at Alamagordo, New Mexico, which he witnessed in the open 10,000 yards from ground zero.

On discharge, Fitch went to McGill University to complete his undergraduate degree; then moved to Columbia for his Ph.D. He spent his career at Princeton University. In 1980 he was awarded the Nobel Prize for physics "for the discovery of violations of fundamental symmetry principles in the decay of neutral K-mesons."

Other future Nobel laureates had a more direct experience of war. Renato Dulbecco served on the Eastern Front in World War II, and subsequently in the Italian Resistance before beginning his scientific career.

Dulbecco was born in Southern Italy in 1914. The family moved north when the father was drafted into the army, and then at the end of the war moved to Imperia, Liguria, where Dulbecco went to school. He spent much time on the beach and in a small meteorological observatory. He built a radio when he was twelve, and later one of the first functioning electronic seismographs, and developed an enthusiasm for physics.

He graduated from high school at 16 and entered the University of Turin. Although talented in physics and mathematics, he decided to study medicine, partly influenced by an uncle who was a surgeon. He was successful in his studies, but realized that he was more interested in biology than in medicine. He worked with Giuseppe Levi, Professor of Anatomy, in whose laboratory he met two other future Nobel laureates, Salvador Luria and Rita Levi-Montalcini. He completed his medical studies in 1936 at the top of his class, and was drafted for military service as a medical officer.

He was discharged two years later and returned to pathology; but, the respite was brief, as he was called up again after the Second World War began. He served in France and was then sent to the Russian Front. He suffered a dislocated shoulder during the Russian advance on the Don, was hospitalized and sent home. This was fortunate, for 80 per cent of his comrades never returned. After the fall of Mussolini and the German occupation, Dulbecco hid out in a village in Piedmont and joined the Resistance, working as a physician with local partisan units. At this time he also taught himself dentistry. He continued to visit the Institute of Morbid Anatomy in Turin, where he joined in underground political activities and was part of the "Committee for National Liberation" of the City of Turin. He became a member of the first postwar city council, but soon abandoned politics to return to medicine and physics.

Salvador Luria, who had gone to the United States at the beginning of the war, offered Dulbecco a position in his laboratory at Indiana, where James Watson was for a time a colleague. There, Dulbecco's work attracted the attention of Max Delbrück (Medicine 1969), who offered him a position at Caltech, where he moved in 1949. He drove from Indiana to California in the family's old car, and writes, "I was fascinated by the beauty and immensity of the USA and the kindness of its people."

He continued to work at Caltech, then at the Salk Institute, and after a few years at the Imperial Cancer Research Fund Laboratories in London, he ended by commuting between Milan and the Salk Institute. He tells an anecdote of his time at the Salk Institute. Frustrated at the time spent at a faculty meeting debating trivialities, he expostulated, "Let's stop this nonsense," and banged his fist on the table. Immediately, a powerful earthquake occurred.

Renato Dulbecco was awarded the Nobel Prize for Medicine in 1975 for "discoveries concerning the interaction between tumor viruses and the genetic material of the cell."

The success of Heinrich Böll (Literature, 1972) as a writer was preceded by wartime service in the Wehrmacht. He served on the Eastern Front, and was wounded a number of times.

Heinrich Böll was born in 1917 in Cologne, Germany. His father was a cabinetmaker and sculptor; Heinrich was brought up, and remained, a Catholic. He refused to join the Hitler Youth while an adolescent, later remarking:

> My unconquerable (and still unconquered) aversion to the Nazis was not revolt, *they* revolted *me*, repelled me on every level of my existence: conscious *and* instinctive, aesthetic *and* political."

He graduated from high school in 1937, and was apprenticed to a bookseller, but after a year went to work for his father. He began to write poetry and fiction, and in 1939 entered the University of Cologne, where he studied literature and classics. He was called up into the Wehrmacht and served first in Poland and France, and was then invalided back to Germany with dysentery. On leave in March 1942 he married Annemarie Cech, a school teacher. In 1943 he was sent to the Eastern Front. His train was blown up but he escaped with minor injuries. He was sent to the Crimea, and was wounded twice. He was next sent to Romania, where he was wounded more seriously, and recovered in a military hospital in Hungary. Toward the end of the war he deserted the army and survived for a time on false papers, before rejoining a reserve regiment. Each time he endeavored to escape the army he was forced back by events. Eventually he was captured by the Americans and sent to a prisoner of war camp. He was released when he feigned illness and returned to Cologne in September 1945.

Böll studied at the University of Cologne and his writing began to be published, but not widely read. His first novel was published in 1949. He worked for some time in the family workshop but from 1951 devoted himself full-time to writing. His early work focused on the misery of soldiers' lives and the cruelties he had witnessed in the army. His first critical and commercial success came in 1953 with the novel *And Never Said a Word*. Other well-known books include *Billiards at Half-past Nine*, *The Clown*, and *Group Portrait with Lady*. He became one of Germany's most-read authors. His novels attempt to come to grips with the Nazi era and the Holocaust and the issue of German guilt. They express compassion for the victims of society and condemn materialism and the forces that led to the German catastrophe. Böll was awarded the Nobel Prize for Literature in 1972. Always aware of the political and social effect of writing and of art, he stated in his Nobel lecture:

> Art is always a good hiding-place, not for dynamite, but for intellectual explosives and social time bombs. What other reason could there have been for all those Indexes of the Church? And it is precisely because of its despised and sometimes even despicable beauty and opacity that art is the best hiding place for that barbed hook that prompts the sudden jolt or the sudden enlightenment.

Heinrich Böll died in 1985 at the age of 67.

A different kind of war was experienced by Malala Yousafzi, the war of fundamentalist Moslem extremism against the rest of the world. Malala`s family run a chain of schools is Swat, Northwestern Pakistan. This was and is an area where the Taliban was active, and where they blew up more than 100 schools. At a young age, Malala became a spokesperson for the right of girls and women to an education; she wrote an anonymous blog, was interviewed for a documentary by the New York Times, and was nominated by Desmond Tutu for the Children`s Peace Prize. On 9 October 2012, a gunman boarded her school bus and shot her in the head. The bullet hit her in the left forehead, and travelled the length of her face and neck into her shoulder. She was treated first in Peshawar and then in Britain. She was in a coma for eight days, but ultimately made a good recovery, with the help of a titanium plate and a cochlear implant. The attack was denounced worldwide, as well as by a group of 50 Pakistani clerics. Malala was deluged with awards and honors. She met Queen Elizabeth and President Obama spoke at Harvard, Oxford, and the United Nations, always with singular dignity and eloquence. On December 10, 2014, she became the youngest Nobel laureate, at 17, when she received the Peace Prize in Oslo. Malala is continuing her education and her activism in Britain.

The first half of the 20th century was an era of war, exile, and slaughter. These same attributes have marked the beginning the 21st century. We may take some comfort from the fact that among those directly affected by these events have been men and women who overcame their experiences to produce great works of science and literature, and great efforts in the cause of peace.

Chapter 21
Never Shall I Forget
These Things

We can never know how many men and women of genius perished in the Holocaust. Two Nobel writers who survived the terrible experiences of the Nazi concentration camps were Elie Wiesel (Peace 1986) and Imre Kertész (Literature, 2002). Elie Wiesel was born in Romania in 1928, the son of an orthodox Jewish shopkeeper. In May 1944, the family was deported to Auschwitz. Elie's mother and younger sister perished there:

> Never shall I forget that night, the first night in camp, which has turned my life into one long night, seven times cursed and seven times sealed.
> Never shall I forget that smoke.
> Never shall I forget the little faces of the children, whose bodies I saw turned into wreaths of smoke beneath a silent blue sky.
> Never shall I forget those flames which consumed my faith forever.
> Never shall I forget that nocturnal silence which deprived me, for all eternity, of the desire to live.
> Never shall I forget those moments which murdered my God and my soul and turned my dreams to dust.
> Never shall I forget these things, even if I am condemned to live as long as God Himself.
> Never!

Wiesel was forced to witness the slow death of his father from mistreatment, starvation, and brutal overwork. His two older sisters survived. In April 1945, Wiesel, then in Buchenwald, was liberated by the American Third Army.

Wiesel moved to Paris, where he studied at the Sorbonne, taught Hebrew and worked as a choirmaster, and then became a professional journalist, writing for Israeli and French newspapers. However, he declined to write or speak about his experiences during the Holocaust. A meeting with François Mauriac (Literature, 1952), the French writer, in 1952, persuaded him to write about his experiences. He wrote first a 245-page memoir in Yiddish that was published in Buenos Aires. Then he produced a shorter version, a 127-page autobiography, *Night*. He had difficulty finding a publisher, and at first it sold few copies. It was published in the US in 1960, but sold only 1046 copies in the next 18 months. The first printing of 3000 copies took three years to sell. But it gradually began to attract attention; by 2008, it was estimated that ten million copies had been sold.

In 1955, Wiesel moved to New York City and became a US citizen. He wrote over forty books of fiction and non-fiction, including a number of volumes of autobiography. He served as chairman of the Presidential Commission on the Holocaust from 1978 to 1986 that spearheaded the building of the Holocaust Memorial Museum in Washington. In 1986 the Nobel Peace Prize was awarded to Wiesel, who was described as "a messenger to mankind: his message is one of peace, atonement and human dignity." Wiesel defines his life's work as a struggle against forgetting and indifference:

> The opposite of love is not hate; it's indifference. The opposite of art is not ugliness; it's indifference. The opposite of faith is not heresy; it's indifference. And the opposite of life is not death; it's indifference.

Imre Kertész was born in Budapest in 1929. At the age of 14, he was deported with other Hungarian Jews to Auschwitz. He was transferred to Buchenwald, where he stayed until liberated in 1945. In his Nobel Acceptance Speech, he elucidated the effect of his concentration camp experience:

> I have endeavoured—perhaps it is not sheer self-deception—to perform the existential labour that being an Auschwitz-survivor has thrust upon me as a kind of obligation. I realize what a privilege has been bestowed on me. I have seen the true visage of this dreadful century; I have gazed into the eye of the Gorgon, and have been able to keep on living. Yet, I knew I would never be able to free myself from the sight; I knew this visage would always hold me captive... And if you now ask me what still

keeps me here on this earth, what keeps me alive; then, I would answer without any hesitation: love.

Kertész had some novel things to say about the Auschwitz experience:

> I experienced my most radical moments of happiness in the concentration camp. You cannot imagine what it's like to be allowed to lie in the camp's hospital, or to have a 10-minute break from indescribable labor. To be very close to death is also a kind of happiness. Just surviving becomes the greatest freedom of all.

On returning to Hungary, he worked for a few years at the newspaper Világosság, but in 1951, after the paper adopted a more orthodox Communist line, he was fired and was drafted for two years of military service. He then lived in Budapest and Berlin, supporting himself as an independent writer and a translator of German-language literature, including works by Canetti, Freud, and Nietzsche. He also wrote musicals and light pieces for the theatre. Not owning a typewriter, he wrote by hand. Aware that his writing, unsympathetic to the communist regime, was un-publishable, he felt that he had the freedom to write as radically as he chose, dependent neither on official approval or public acclaim.

His first published book, *Sostalandság*, which was completed in 1965 but not published until ten years later, was an account of a fifteen year old Jewish boy's experiences in concentration camps. It was published in a limited edition, and greeted with silence. This was followed by two books in which the protagonist is a middle aged survivor of the Holocaust. However, Kertész remained largely unknown as a writer until the fall of the Soviet Union, when both his reputation and his publication increased. In 2002 he was awarded the Nobel Prize in Literature, "for writing that upholds the fragile experience of the individual against the barbaric arbitrariness of history."

Another Jewish laureate, who survived the Nazi rule in Europe, was Daniel Kahneman; he lived through World War II in France. In his Nobel autobiography, he tells an anecdote from his childhood:

Jews were required to wear the Star of David and to obey a 6 p.m. curfew. I had gone to play with a Christian friend and had stayed too late. I turned my brown sweater inside out to walk the few blocks home. As I was walking down an empty street, I saw a German soldier approaching. He was wearing the black uniform that I had been told to fear more than others—the one worn by specially recruited SS soldiers. As I came closer to him, trying to walk fast, I noticed that he was looking at me intently. Then he beckoned me over, picked me up, and hugged me. I was terrified that he would notice the star inside my sweater. He was speaking to me with great emotion, in German. When he put me down, he opened his wallet, showed me a picture of a boy, and gave me some money. I went home more certain than ever that my mother was right: people were endlessly complicated and interesting.

Some Jews avoided both emigration and the concentration camps by going into hiding, and this was the case with Rita Levi-Montalcini. As a young woman, against her father's wishes, she enrolled in medical school in Turin. She graduated *summa cum laude* in medicine and surgery, and entered a three-year specialization in neurology and psychiatry. In 1936 Mussolini passed racial laws banning non-Aryans from professional careers. Rita built a research laboratory in her bedroom where she undertook studies of the development of chick embryos. When heavy bombing of Turin made a move necessary, the family moved to a country cottage where Rita rebuilt her lab in the kitchen and resumed her experiments. The invasion of Italy by the Germans in 1943 made this existence too dangerous, and for the rest of the war the family lived underground in Florence. When the Germans were expelled from Florence, Rita worked as a doctor with refugees among whom disease was epidemic. When the Germans left Italy, she resumed her work at the University of Turin. Subsequently, she divided her time between Washington University in St. Louis and a research unit she established in Rome. Levi-Montalcini was awarded the Nobel Prize for Medicine in 1986. At her one hundredth birthday party, she dispensed this advice: "Above all, don't fear difficult moments. The best comes from them."

The experiences of Nobel laureates seem to confirm the conclusions reached by Victor Frankl and published in his book, *Man's Search for*

Meaning (2006). Meaning in life is achieved by one or more of three avenues: by doing a deed, by experiencing something or encountering someone, or by the attitude we take toward unavoidable suffering. This philosophy, logotherapy, was worked out by Frankl while he was a prisoner for three years in Auschwitz.

Chapter 22
Without Luck, Forget it

How much of success can be accounted for by luck, and how much luck is required for success? Mihaly Csikszentmihalyi and his colleagues interviewed 91 highly creative people, including several Nobel laureates:

> When we asked creative persons what explains their success, one of the most frequent answers—perhaps the most frequent one— was that they were lucky. Being in the right place at the right time is an almost universal explanation.

Nobel laureates would agree with this. They generally have the luck to be born into families that can provide them with, or guide them to, the educational resources they need. They have luck in the colleagues and mentors they work with, and they have luck in their choice of field of endeavor and in their discoveries.

Francis Crick said of the discovery of the double helix, "We were jolly lucky… and very stupid. The problem was quite easy."

Max Delbrück said, "If you are lucky and persistent you may make fantastic discoveries."

Early in the 20th century, Paul Ehrlich (Medicine 1908) said, "Success in research needs four G's: Glück, Geduld, Geschick, and Geld." (luck, patience, skill, and money).

In *The Old Man and the Sea*, Hemingway observes that: "It is better to be lucky, but I would rather be exact. Then when luck comes, you are ready."

Roger Kornberg (Chemistry 2006) said: "Do whatever you do just as well as you possibly can. After that, some people get lucky."

Richard Roberts (Medicine 1993) said, "Ask good questions. Ask big questions. Look for things that are unusual. The key is to take advantage of luck when it comes along."

Leon Lederman was explicit:

Without luck, forget it. If you don't have incandescent good fortune, don't be a scientist. You need luck, because a career in science is full of mistakes, bad judgments, missed opportunities, experiments that failed because the equipment doesn't work. That's part of the game. So if you want to be a successful scientist, better make sure you have luck.

It was pure luck that the spores of penicillin blew on to Alexander Fleming's (Medicine, 1945) *petri* dishes; but it was insight, not luck, that enabled him to recognize what he saw.

As Louis Pasteur said, "Fortune favors the prepared mind."

Chapter 23
So I Stopped Wearing Socks

In the public mind, a genius is expected to be eccentric. Einstein once remarked, "When I was young, I found out that the big toe always ends up making a hole in a sock. So I stopped wearing socks."

Einstein was marked by such mild eccentricities. But he was an exception. What strikes the reader of the lives of Nobel laureates is their general down-to-earth common sense and lack of pretension. An extreme degree of eccentricity would probably be a disqualification for the Nobel Prize. Nevertheless, there were some laureates who were at least as eccentric as Einstein.

Paul Dirac was a man of very few words. On a visit to the United States, he was asked by a reporter what he liked best about America. His response: "Potatoes."

He put his reticence down to the fact that although he grew up in England, his father, who was Swiss, insisted that he speak French at home. He was famously exact in his speech. At the end of one of his lectures, he called for questions. A member of the audience said he didn't understand a part of the lecture. Dirac ignored him. When prompted by the chairman, he said, "That is not a question, it's a statement." When he was visiting a castle in Denmark he was told that a ghost appeared nightly at midnight; he asked, "Is that midnight Greenwich time or daylight saving time?" He once declined some books offered him by the physicist Richard Oppenheimer, remarking that reading books interfered with thought. He said on several occasions that it was more important that an equation be beautiful than that it fit experimental data. Niels Bohr said of him, "Of all physicists, Dirac has the purest soul." In his last years, Paul Dirac lived in Florida. When invited to give a talk at the University of Florida, he replied, "No! I have nothing to talk about. My life has been a failure."

Kary Mullis won the Nobel Prize for Medicine in 1993 "for his invention of the polymerase chain reaction (PCR) method". When the telephone call came from Stockholm early in the morning, he was slow to answer it and the caller had hung up.

> Almost instantly the phone rang again. He had heard me just as he'd hung up. "Congratulations, Dr. Mullis. I am pleased to be able to announce to you that you have been awarded the Nobel Prize." "I'll take it!" I said."

The party celebrating the prize went on for two days.

> Eventually it moved north to my place in Mendocino. Roederer Vineyards was just down the road, and no one failed to notice. I woke up late one afternoon from a dream that I was dead in a coffin. Winning the Nobel Prize can be hazardous to your health.

Mullis had been concerned that the Nobel Committee might look askance at three of his main interests, surfing, women, and LSD. When asked what he did with the prize money, he said, "As Yogi Berra, who had also won a substantial prize, said, I spent most of it on women and alcohol, and the rest of it, I wasted."

In his autobiography, *Dancing Naked in the Mind Field*, Mullis expresses scepticism regarding global warming, the hole in the ozone layer, and the connection between HIV and AIDS. He is also sceptical of diet gurus, saying, "Some people eat too much, some people eat too little. Nothing else about diet really matters." He describes a period of several hours of amnesia he experienced, during which, he speculates, he was abducted by aliens.

Mullis, however, stands out as an exception among the body of Nobel laureates. Their lives tend to be unexceptional; it is their thinking that is idiosyncratic. It is self-evident that new discoveries will not be made by following conventional wisdom. Dissent, not compliance, is the mark of the pioneer.

This was stressed by André Geim (Physics, 2011) in his Nobel banquet speech, in which he issued a warning about the pressure of conventional thinking:

> Human progress has always been driven by a sense of adventure and unconventional thinking. But amidst calls for "bread and circuses", these virtues are often forgotten for the sake of

cautiousness and political correctness that now rule the world. And we sink deeper and deeper from democracy into a state of mediocrity and even idiocracy.

We could say of the entire Nobel project that it strikes a blow against the forces of idiocracy.

Chapter 24
Bloody Disaster

For Nobel laureates, the measure of success is not the prize itself, but the work that led up to it. Many laureates view the Nobel Prize as a mixed blessing. Doris Lessing said it was "A bloody disaster… All I do is give interviews and spend time being photographed."

T. S. Eliot is well known for having said that "The Nobel is a ticket to one's own funeral. No one has ever done anything after he got it."

Saul Bellow (Literature, 1976) called it the "kiss of death" for a writer.

Jacques Monod declared that "The Prize is very good for science and very bad for the scientists."

Daniel McFadden (Economics, 2000) warned, "If you're not careful, the Nobel Prize is a career-ender. If I allowed myself to slip into it, I'd spend all my time going around cutting ribbons."

Torsten Wiesel was told that he'd won the prize for medicine in 1981, he said, "Oh, no, I was afraid of that! I better go and hide."

Sinclair Lewis (Literature, 1930) declared "This is the end of me. This is fatal. I cannot live up to it."

Isaac Bashevis Singer (Literature, 1978) was much more restrained. After the early morning phone call from Stockholm, he said to his wife, "In any case, let's eat breakfast."

Maria Mayer said, "If you love science, all you really want is to keep on working. The Nobel Prize thrills you, but it changes nothing."

José Saramago (Literature, 1998) described the experience of winning the Nobel Prize as "like being hit on the head, but not hard enough to make you fall down. You carry on walking around and wait to come back to your senses."

When the peace prize was awarded in 1973 to Henry Kissinger and Le Duc Tho, who were negotiating an end to the war in Vietnam, the vote in the Committee was 3-2, and the two dissenting members resigned. Kissinger was identified more with the war than with the peace, and peace had not in fact yet been achieved. On the latter ground, Le Duc Tho refused the prize and took no part in the ceremonies. Kissinger did not attend the prize giving either, and was represented by the United States ambassador to Norway. Subsequently, when peace proved elusive, Kissinger enquired whether he could return the prize, but was informed that there was no procedure for doing so.

The Nobel Prize is one of the few honors where the consent of recipients is not sought prior to the award. Nevertheless, there are very few cases of refusal.

Eric Karlfeldt, a Swedish writer, was secretary of the Swedish Academy, and a member of the Nobel Committee. He refused the prize for literature in 1918, because it would have required him to resign from these positions. He was awarded the prize posthumously, after his death in 1931.

Jean-Paul Sartre rejected the prize when it was awarded to him in 1964. In his letter to the Nobel committee, he wrote:

> I have always declined official distinctions. When, after the war, in 1945, I was nominated for the Legion of Honor I refused... It is not the same thing if I sign Jean-Paul Sartre or if I sign Jean-Paul Sartre Nobel Prize. The writer, then, must refuse to let himself be transformed into an institution.

According to Lars Gyllensten, a member of the Nobel Prize committee for many years, Sartre, who was notoriously bad at managing money, eleven years later, he wrote to the Nobel committee asking if he could now receive the prize money; the committee turned him down.

After Von Ossietzky was awarded the Peace Prize in 1935, Hitler forbade Germans to accept the Nobel Prize. Three German laureates, Richard Kuhn (Chemistry 1938), Adolf Butenandt (Chemistry 1939) and Gerhard Domagk (Medicine 1939) had to wait until after the war to collect their prizes.

The only other refusal was by Boris Pasternak, who was awarded the prize in 1958. At first he accepted it gratefully, telegraphing the Committee, "Immensely thankful, touched, proud, astonished, abashed." But because his major novel, *Dr. Zhivago*, first published in Italy after rejection in the USSR, was considered critical of the Soviet Union, he became subject to enormous pressure from the Soviet government, including the threat of expulsion from the country. Soviet authorities denounced the award as being "a purely political act hostile to our country and aimed at intensifying the Cold War." Pasternak sent a second telegram to Stockholm: "Considering the meaning this award has been given in the society to which I belong, I must refuse it. Please do not take offense at my voluntary rejection." Pasternak was repeatedly attacked in the Soviet press, and was expelled from the Union of Soviet Writers. He died in 1960 from heart disease, and a few weeks later his close friend, Olga Ivinskaya, was charged with currency violations and sentenced to eight years in labor camp; her daughter received a sentence of three years. Both were sent to Siberia.

An interesting footnote was provided to these events in 2007. Ivan Tolstoy, a writer based in Prague, where he worked for Radio Free Europe and Radio Liberty, announced that he had discovered the role of the CIA in Pasternak's award, and would publish it in a forthcoming book. According to Tolstoy, the CIA obtained a typescript of the novel in Russian from an air passenger's luggage, copied and replaced it, and then had it published in Holland, in order to meet the Nobel regulation that works by laureates must be available in the language in which they were written. This account has been disputed by others, including the Slavic scholar Lazar Fleishman.

What do the winners do with the prize money? In most cases, we don't know. Albert Camus built a country house, Richard Feynman a beach house. The Joliot-Curies built a big house in a Paris suburb. Lord Rayleigh gave it to Cambridge University to extend the Cavendish Laboratory. Bernard Shaw refused the money and asked for it to be used to establish an Anglo-Swedish Literary Foundation. Gunter Blobel gave it to the city of Dresden to rebuild the Frauenkirche there and to build a new synagogue. He and his family had been "received with open arms" by the people of Dresden at the end of the war when they were fleeing westward. The gift was also in memory of his sister Ruth, who was killed in the last days of the war. Martin Luther King donated the prize money to the civil rights movement. Paul Greengard (Medicine 2000) gave the money to Rockefeller University to establish a fund to provide an annual prize for an outstanding woman doing biomedical research. He said, "My mother died in childbirth. I never knew her. And it seemed a very nice way to honor her memory."

Chapter 25
Controversial Nobels

The success that Nobel laureates achieve in winning the Prize is not always universally acknowledged. This is particularly the case with the Peace prizes. During the Cold War, whenever a Soviet dissident was honored, the Soviet press would attack the prize as a Cold War provocation. When the choice was unpopular in America, the press there would attack the award as anti-American. Under J. Edgar Hoover, who hated Martin Luther King with a passion, the FBI warned King not to go to Oslo to receive the award, but rather to commit suicide, on pain of having details of his extramarital affairs revealed to the media.

The discovery of insulin is normally attributed to Banting and Best. But Banting and Macleod got the Nobel. Frederick Banting had originally entered the University of Toronto to study divinity, but soon switched to medicine. He graduated in 1916, joined the army, was wounded at Cambrai, and received the Military Cross for gallantry under fire. On his return to Canada, he started a general practice, while studying orthopedics and lecturing on pharmacology. He also became interested in diabetes. It was known that diabetics lacked insulin, which metabolized sugar, leading to an excess of sugar in the blood. The problem was how to extract insulin without it first being destroyed by the proteolytic enzyme in the pancreas. He discussed this problem with a number of people, including Dr. John Macleod, director of the physiology laboratory, who provided him with laboratory space where he was assisted by a medical student, Charles Best. At about 2:00 AM of the morning of 30 October 1920, Banting wrote himself a memo: "Ligate pancreatic ducts of dogs. Keep dogs alive till acini degenerate leaving Islets." This procedure proved successful, enabling the experimenters to extract insulin undamaged, which could subsequently be provided to diabetics. The discovery was announced in February 1922 and immediately celebrated as a medical breakthrough, and in 1923 Frederick Banting was awarded the Nobel Prize in medicine. He shared the prize with Macleod. Macleod had in fact had little to do with the discovery other than provide laboratory space; he was on vacation at the time of the discovery.

Banting and Macleod were both nominated by August Krogh (Medicine 1920), who had visited Toronto and attested that Macleod's aid and supervision had been critical to the discovery. Banting was appalled by the omission of Charles Best (who had not been nominated), and divided his prize money with him. Banting went on to have a distinguished career in medicine. In World War II, he served as a liaison officer between British and North American medical services. He wrote in his diary on 31 January 1941, "Never was there a time in my life when I had so much to live for—and so much to die for." Three weeks later he was killed in a plane crash in Newfoundland.

Fritz Haber invented poison gas for the German army in World War I. In 1918 he was awarded a Nobel Prize by Sweden. In 1919 he was declared a war criminal by Britain. Haber's father was a businessman who owned a chemical works, where his son worked briefly before committing himself to a scientific career. Prior to World War I, Haber discovered the means of making ammonia from the air. This was a discovery of enormous importance. Ammonia was critical to the manufacture of nitrates, of which Germany had no natural sources; without it, a necessary ingredient of explosives, the German war machine would have ground to a halt a few months into World War I. Without nitrogen fertilizers, the Green Revolution would have been impossible, and the world could not support its present population. It was this discovery for which the Nobel Prize honored Haber. He was appointed head of the chemical warfare department during the war, managing an industrial enterprise employing 1500 people. With respect to gas warfare, he warned in 1914, "If there is even the remotest possibility that the war will last beyond the summer of 1915, reject all schemes for gas warfare. If you disregard my warning, we shall be beaten by the use of our own weapons." The British and French quickly developed poison gas weapons.

He was assisted by several other leading German scientists including the future Nobel laureates, James Franck (Physics 1925) and Otto Hahn (Chemistry 1944). During one of his home leaves, his wife, who was the first woman to gain a Ph.D. at the University of Breslau, shot herself with his service revolver. Her motivation remains obscure, there is little evidence that this act was in protest against Haber's work in gas warfare, and more likely had to do with her own nervous condition and stresses in the marriage.

After the war, Haber worked for normalization in relations with the Allied countries. He argued that "A scientist belongs to his country in times of war and to all mankind in times of peace." He continued active in chemical research, producing several important inventions and discoveries. He served on the League of Nations Committee on chemical warfare. He was appointed Director of the Kaiser Wilhelm Institute for Physical Chemistry and Electrochemistry at Berlin in 1911. He continued in this post until the advent of the Nazis. Then, when ordered to expel Jewish professors (he himself was Jewish, but was excluded from the order on account of his war service), he resigned. In his letter of resignation, he wrote:

> I tender my resignation with the same pride with which I have served my country during my lifetime... For more than forty years I have selected my collaborators on the basis of their intelligence and their character and not on the basis of their grandmothers, and I am not willing to change, for the rest of my life this method which I have found so good.

He left Germany for Britain. He wrote to a friend, "The life's work I have lost is for me irreplaceable." Unwilling to endure a winter in Britain, already suffering from heart disease, and broken in spirit, he departed for Israel, where he had long had a standing invitation. But he died en route in Switzerland in 1934.

Philipp Lenard, who won the Nobel Prize for physics in 1905, became Chief of Aryan Physics under the Nazis. His Nobel Prize was awarded "for his work in connection with cathode rays". He also made significant discoveries in the areas of the structure of atoms, falling drop theory, magnetism and luminescence, and the understanding of spectral lines. He distrusted English physics, believing that it was largely stolen from German sources. He was a lifelong anti-Semite, and an early adherent of the Nazi party. He opposed what he called "Jewish physics," referring mainly to Einstein and the theory of relativity. In 1945, at the age of 83, he was expelled by Allied forces from his position as professor emeritus at Heidelberg University, and died two years later.

Another admirer of Adolf Hitler was Knut Hamsun, the Norwegian writer who won the prize for literature in 1920. Hamsun grew up in poverty, and worked at various low-paying jobs. He spent some years in America, where he worked as a tram driver in Chicago, later publishing his satirical impressions in the book, *The Intellectual Life of Modern America* (1889). His novels *Hunger* (1890) and *Pan* (1894) made him famous. In addition to novels, he wrote plays and poetry. His work is marked by an aversion to civilization and a belief that humanity is best suited to work with the soil. His work introduced modernist fiction to Norway. Isaac Bashevis Singer went further, stating in 1967 that "the whole school of fiction in the 20th century stems from Hamsun."

Hamsun was a lifelong Anglophobe and Germanophile. He supported Germany in both the First and Second World Wars, and was an opponent of British imperialism and of the Soviet Union. He welcomed the German invasion of Norway in 1940 and the pro-German Quisling government. In 1943 he visited Germany, and expressed his appreciation to his host, Josef Goebbels, by sending him his Nobel medal. During this visit he had a 45-minute audience with Adolf Hitler. By now quite deaf, he held forth on Norwegian affairs with such vehemence that Hitler, for once, could not get a word in. When Hamsun left, Hitler ordered his staff never to admit him again. After Hitler's death, Hamsun wrote an obituary for a collaborationist newspaper, in which he declared that Hitler "was a warrior, a warrior for mankind, and a prophet of the gospel of justice for all nations."

At the end of the war, Hamsun was arrested on charges of treason. He was placed in a mental hospital, and was deemed to be suffering from "permanently impaired mental abilities", on which grounds the charges against him were dropped. All his property was confiscated, and he died in poverty in 1952 at the age of 92. With time, Norwegian views of Hamsun have softened, and while his Nazi associations are not forgotten, his 150th birthday in 2009 was commemorated with exhibitions, a museum, a postage stamp, and a statue of Hamsun.

Other laureates provide evidence that the Nobel Prize is not awarded for perfection. T. S. Eliot (Literature 1948) and Jose Saramago (Literature 1998) both expressed unforgivable anti-Semitic sentiments. Jean-Paul Sartre (Literature 1964) and Mikhail Sholokhov (Literature 1965) were pro-Stalinists; and Charles Richet (Medicine 1913) was a blatant racist.

Egas Moniz, a Portuguese neurosurgeon, won the Nobel Prize for medicine in 1949 for inventing the prefrontal lobotomy. Born in 1874,

Antonio Caetana de Abreu Freire Egas Moniz earned his medical degree in 1899. He published one of the first textbooks on sexual pathology, and was the originator of cerebral angiography. He was elected to Parliament in 1911, and served as Portugal's Ambassador to Spain and then as Foreign Minister, leaving politics after fighting a duel with a political opponent. In 1939 he was shot in his office by a schizophrenic patient, and spent the rest of his life in a wheelchair. He died in 1955.

Now that lobotomy is all but discredited, and mental illness is treated by a wide range of psychotropic drugs, it is not easy to imagine conditions in the 1940s, when the mentally ill were dealt with by methods that were crude and brutal. Restraints, in the form of chains or straitjackets, were frequently used, and therapy included such treatments as ice-cold baths, heavy sedation, or induced insulin coma. Nearly half of all hospital beds in the United States were occupied by mental patients in 1946, and institutionalized mental patients had high rates of tuberculosis and other infectious diseases.

In the lobotomy, called at the time leucotomy, the patient is first anesthetised, usually by a series of electroconvulsive shocks, then a stainless steel probe with a retractable arm is pushed through the bone above the eyeball and rotated to sever the connections between the prefrontal lobe and the rest of the brain. In his first experiments in 1937, Moniz found that some patients experienced remission of psychotic symptoms, although the most severe cases and schizophrenics did not appear to benefit. It was noted by others that the surgery rendered patients passive and listless. A study of 10,365 lobotomies conducted in Britain from 1942 to 1954 showed that 41% had recovered or were greatly improved, 25% were minimally improved, 2% showed no change, 2% had deteriorated, and 4% had died.

In 1952, the first tranquillizer, chlorpromazine, was introduced, and quickly became the treatment of choice for affective disorders, while ECT had become widely used in the treatment of depression. Lobotomy fell out of fashion, although it is still used occasionally in Sweden today.

As previously mentioned, controversy over Nobel Prizes has most frequently occurred with respect to the Peace Prize. Even the first prize, in 1901, to Henri Dunant, founder of the Red Cross, and Frédéric Passy, a leading member of the peace movement, caused debate. Nobel's will called for the prize to be awarded to the person who "shall have done the most or the best work for fraternity between nations, for the abolition or reduction of standing armies and for the holding of peace congresses." Those who thought Passy should have been honored alone asked what the Red Cross did for the prevention of war. As the peace prize evolved, however, it came to be used to recognize those engaged in humanitarian work, in work for civil rights, and more recently for environmental activism.

Theodore Roosevelt received the peace prize in 1906, for his work in negotiating peace between Japan and Russia. The *New York Times* referred to Roosevelt as "the most warlike citizen of these United States," and Roosevelt was in fact probably the most bellicose of all US Presidents. "All the great masterful races have been fighting races" he once declared. The advisor to the Nobel Committee averred that Roosevelt's role in detaching Panama from Colombia had violated international law. On the other hand, Roosevelt initiated the work of the International Court of Arbitration by bringing to it a dispute between the United States and Mexico. He also concluded several arbitration agreements with European states.

One of the most controversial Nobel Peace Prizes was awarded to Yasser Arafat in 1994. He, Shimon Peres, and Yitzak Rabin were awarded the prize for their negotiations leading to the Oslo Accords between Israel and the Palestinian people. The objection to Arafat was that he had been a terrorist under whose chairmanship of the Palestine Liberation Organization many Israeli civilian lives had been taken. In the course of the negotiations leading to the Oslo Accords, Arafat renounced violence and recognized Israel's right to exist. Prime Minister Rabin, on Israel's behalf, officially recognized the PLO. One member of the Nobel Committee, Kaare Kristiansen, leader of the Norwegian Christian Democratic Party, resigned in protest over the award.

At Ladbrooke's, the British turf accountant, one can lay bets on the current year's Nobel Prize winner in literature. It is unlikely that many people have become rich by this means. Part of the appeal of the Nobel Prizes is their unpredictability, and this is reinforced by the secrecy of the Committees' deliberations. Controversy is the price of refusing the obvious and the conventional.

Chapter 26
Over my Dead Body

Public success requires not only achievement but recognition. A book could be written on individuals who merited the Nobel Prize but did not receive it. In 1901, the first year the prize was awarded many people felt strongly that Leo Tolstoy should have received the prize for literature, rather than the now-forgotten French writer, Sully Prudhomme. In fact, Tolstoy had not been nominated; in that first year, only 25 nominations were received, mostly from France. A group of more than 40 Swedish writers and artists wrote to Tolstoy expressing their admiration for his work and regret that he had not been recognized by the Nobel committee. Tolstoy died in 1910, never winning the Nobel award, while it went to a series of writers, many of whom are now judged to be Tolstoy's inferiors. During the early years, the Committee interpreted the phrase in Nobel's will: "of an idealistic tendency" to mean "a lofty and sound idealism," which excluded agnostics, materialists, and sensualists. The members of the committee were deterred by Tolstoy's anarchism and his eccentric religious views. A 1905 Committee report remarked that Tolstoy "in countless of his works denies not only the church but the state, even the right of property." Tolstoy claimed to be undismayed: "It saved me from the painful necessity of dealing in some way with money, which I regard as the source of every kind of evil."

The list of those who did not receive the literature prize includes: Mark Twain, Henrik Ibsen, Maxim Gorky, Paul Valery, Thomas Hardy, George Meredith, Joseph Conrad, Rainer Maria Rilke, Vladimir Nabokov, Lawrence Durrell, André Malraux, C. P. Cavafy, D. H. Lawrence, Osip Mandelstam, Nikos Kazantzakis, James Joyce, Marcel Proust, Anton Chekhov, Berthold Brecht, Virginia Woolf, Jorge Luis Borges, and Graham Greene.

A leading member of the Nobel Committee, Dr. Artur Lundkvist, disapproved of Graham Greene. "Greene is too popular," he said. "He doesn't need the money." He was also reported as saying, "Graham Greene will receive the Nobel Prize over my dead body."

Ernest Hemingway was awarded the Nobel Prize for literature in 1954, after being passed over several times. According to Lyle Larson, the award was a tribute by the Nobel committee to a senior member, Per Hallstrom, who was an admirer of Hemingway, and was retiring from the committee at the age of 89.

Sigmund Freud was never awarded the Nobel Prize for Medicine. An internal report of the committee commented that he was "At the mercy of a sick and distorted imagination" to a greater extent than his patients.

Equally controversial was the non-award of the peace prize to Mahatma Gandhi. After being nominated in several previous years, he made it on to the Committee's short list in 1947. Two members of the committee strongly supported Gandhi's candidacy, but could not persuade the other three. Opposition came from the fact that India and Pakistan were in the midst of the turmoil of partition, and Gandhi was identified with one side in the conflict. Furthermore, a telegram from Reuters, which became the basis of an article in *The Times* on September 27, 1947, appeared to indicate that Gandhi was retreating from his policy of non-violence in the Indo-Pakistan conflict. The report was later shown to be incomplete. Gandhi was assassinated on January 30, 1948, two days before the closing date for that year's Nobel Peace Prize nominations. Gandhi received six nominations. The Committee considered a posthumous award, but ultimately rejected the idea. At that time there was no formal rule against posthumous awards, but there were practical obstacles in that Gandhi belonged to no organization and left no will; who would receive the prize money? In the end, the committee did not award a peace prize in 1948 on the grounds that "there was no suitable living candidate"

It is unusual for those passed over for the Nobel Prize to complain publicly, but this occurred in 2003. In that year, the award went to Paul Lauterbur and Peter Mansfield "for their discoveries involving magnetic resonance imaging." Dr. Raymond Damadian took out full-page advertisements in the American press complaining that his contribution to MRI had been overlooked. His alma mater, the University of Wisconsin-Madison had in 1998 given him an honorary doctorate as "one of the inventors of magnetic resonance imaging," he had filed the first patent on medical use of MRI, and he developed the first commercial MR scanner. The consensus of medical opinion, however, was that the Nobel Committee's decision had been the correct one.

Chapter 27
The Secret of their Success

The preceding chapters have suggested a range of factors that facilitate the success of Nobel laureates. Family background, education, the help of mentors and collaborators, a stable family, intelligence and intuition, perseverance, and luck all play a part. But none of these factors is indispensable. Nor are the experiences of imprisonment, war, or exile insuperable obstacles. We have yet to isolate a factor that is essential to the success of all Nobel laureates. Even Nobel laureates find this difficult to pin down. Jack Szostak, who won the Prize for Medicine in 2009, writes in his Nobel biography:

> I greatly enjoy reading the biographies of scientists, and when doing so I always hope to learn the secrets of their success. Alas, those secrets generally remain elusive. Now that I find myself in the surprising situation of having to write my own biography, and thus to reflect on my career, I find the same mystery.

But there is a secret, which other laureates have been able to discern. It is what Leon Lederman called "compulsive dedication—the insistence on working without rest until you get what you're after." Marie Curie stirring the cauldron of pitchblende from dawn to dusk; Aleksandr Solzhenitsyn writing books for which he saw no hope of publication; Shirin Ebadi continuing to work for human rights despite imprisonment and death threats; Barry Marshall pursuing his belief in helicobactor pylori in the teeth of establishment skepticism. The careers of these and many other laureates are testimony to their dedication.

At some point in their lives, Nobel laureates develop a passionate attachment to a particular cause, activity, genre of writing, or area of science. Of course, those who become Nobel laureates need also to have the energy required to engage in the labors entailed in their vocation, but several have succeeded despite intermittent ill-health. They also have basic good sense in the decisions they make regarding such things as where and with whom to study, and whom to marry. But it is their passion that distinguishes them, and makes them fellows of all whose hearts as well as their heads are deeply engaged in their chosen field. The Peruvian writer, Mario Vargas Llosa (Literature, 2010), said of his work:

> I know that I'll write until the day I die. Writing is in my nature. I live my life according to my work. If I didn't write, I would blow my brains out, without a shadow of a doubt.

Arthur Kornberg (Chemistry, 1959) put it in a nutshell: "As with other creative endeavors, sustained productivity at a high level in science demands total devotion. I don't know of any exceptions." He explained what lay behind his endeavors:

> I was awed by enzymes and fell instantly in love with them. I have since had love affairs with many enzymes… but I have never met a dull or disappointing one.

Kornberg named his autobiography, *For Love of Enzymes*.

In similar terms, Stanford Moore (Chemistry, 1972) said, "I can imagine no life more fascinating or more rewarding than one spent exploring the elegant and complicated architecture of organic molecules." This kind of emotion accompanies its possessors through the long periods of apprenticeship and the almost inevitable periods of discouragement. It inspires them to seek out mentors and colleagues who share their interests. It is strong enough to enable them to transcend the experiences of discrimination, exile, prison, and rejection by the establishment. And although the work entailed is almost unremitting, it is experienced as pleasure. Late in his life, the Russian biologist Ivan Pavlov (Medicine 1904), said, "I dreamed of finding happiness in intellectual work, in science—and I found it." Speaking to university students in Stockholm, William Fowler (Physics 1983) said:

> Fellow students, there will be hard work and heart break in your futures but there will also be stimulating intellectual pleasure and joy. In less pompous language I call it fun.

Alan MacDiarmid (Chemistry, 2000) said, "One has to live it, eat it, dream it, sleep it. It has to be complete immersion… The creative scientist is just as much an artist as a person composing a symphony or painting a beautiful painting." Alan MacDiarmid became world famous when he won the Nobel Prize for Chemistry in 2000. But he started his scientific career washing bottles in a university laboratory.

MacDiarmid was born in New Zealand in 1927. During the Depression, which affected New Zealand severely, his father, an engineer, was unemployed for four years. MacDiarmid went to school barefoot, to small schools where most of his fellow pupils were Maori. Every morning before grade school he delivered milk; during high school he had a paper route. His interest in science was kindled during this period, first by reading one of his father's old chemistry textbooks, and then by books from the local library. MacDiarmid attributes his success in life to the close and nurturing family in which he grew up.

At the age of 16, MacDiarmid left school and took a low-paying, part-time job as a "lab boy" and janitor in the chemistry department at Victoria University College in Wellington. His tasks included washing lab ware, sweeping floors, and preparing demonstration chemicals. He lived in the university men's dormitory, and took university courses part-time. After earning a B.Sc. he became a demonstrator and went on to earn an M.Sc. In 1950, he received a Fulbright fellowship from the US State Department to do a Ph.D. at the University of Wisconsin. He undertook further study at Cambridge University, and then moved to the University of Pennsylvania, where he spent 43 years. He said once, "I always say that when you stop learning you start dying."

Alan MacDiarmid was awarded the Nobel Prize in Chemistry in 2000, "for the discovery and development of conductive polymers." At the end of his Nobel lecture, he publicly thanked his parents "for providing a loving and solid home foundation on which to base my life." The motto that hangs in his study reads, "I am a very lucky person and the harder I work the luckier I seem to be."

We may examine one final example of outstanding dedication in the life and work of Howard Florey, who, with Ernest Chain and Alexander Fleming, was awarded the Nobel Prize in 1945 for the development of penicillin.

Florey was Australian by birth. He left Australia with a medical degree and a Rhodes scholarship to study at Oxford. From there he went as a professor to Sheffield and then returned to Oxford as Professor of Pathology. He had many publications to his credit on the subject of the role of the cell in inflammation and its effect on tissue, when in 1938 he began to study penicillin.

Penicillin had been discovered by Alexander Fleming in 1929. Fleming left some *petri* dishes containing staphylococci un-cleaned in his lab while he went on holiday. When he returned, he noticed that a mold was growing on some of the dishes, and this mold appeared to be killing the bacteria. He named the mold penicillin, and found that it also killed pneumococcus and streptococcus in vitro, and did no harm to healthy organisms. He used it on a few surface infections with mixed results. Fleming published a couple of papers on the subject, but decided that penicillin was too difficult to isolate or make in quantity to be of practical interest. There the matter rested until Florey came across one of Fleming's papers while researching agents that could be used against bacteria.

At this time, doctors knew the cause of infection, but not the cure. Sulfanomides, discovered in Germany in the early 1930s, were used with variable success. But millions of children still died of infectious diseases, mothers died of puerperal fever or septicemia after giving birth, treatment for gonorrhea and syphilis were painful and only partly effective, wounds and burns were frequently fatal, and a diagnosis of pneumonia, meningitis, diphtheria, or tuberculosis was often a death sentence.

Florey gathered a team of researchers, including the biochemist Ernest Chain, a German refugee (and concert level pianist) working in Cambridge. He had to spend much of his time raising funds for the research, until a generous grant was awarded by the Rockefeller Foundation. Many different growth media were tried before the team had success with brewer's yeast. Then, there was the long struggle to isolate the fraction of penicillin that was active against bacteria. Finally, the right combination of low temperature, acidity level, evaporation in a vacuum chamber, and concentration and re-concentration resulted in a pinch of dirty brown powder, 99% of which was rubbish. The first controlled test was made with eight mice, and was successful. Then followed multiple trials with mice as dosages and timing were worked out.

All of this was being done at the beginning of the Second World War, while Britain was under imminent threat of invasion by Germany. Florey and a colleague decided that if the Germans invaded, they would escape to America, carrying penicillin spores in their clothes. Special vessels had to be made to exact specifications for culturing the penicillin broth. Precautions were necessary to prevent contamination from the air, and the material had to be purified and re-purified. Gradually output increased and stocks accumulated. A couple of abortive trials were made on patients, but results were inconclusive. Then a policeman, dying of a streptococcus infection, experienced a miraculous recovery as a result of administration of penicillin. Unfortunately, after several days of treatment, the penicillin supply ran out, the infection returned, and the patient died.

This early work showed therapeutic promise, and also demonstrated that penicillin was not harmful to humans. It was followed by increasing numbers of successful clinical trials. Florey was unable to interest the British chemical industry in the development of penicillin; so, he traveled to the United States, where several laboratories took up the challenge of manufacturing penicillin in large quantities. Penicillin began to be used to treat burned airmen and wounded American soldiers. Gangrene, which had killed 15% of wounded soldiers in World War I, became a thing of the past. The effect on venereal disease, which previously had taken the equivalent of three divisions out of action, was miraculous. The US Military gave the development of penicillin priority second only to research on the atomic bomb. American manufacturers built 10,000-gallon tanks for fomentation, and penicillin began to be mass produced. It was tried out on troops in North Africa, and was available in quantity for allied troops when they invaded Europe in 1944.

During the early war years, when Florey and his colleagues worked day and night to develop penicillin--overcoming obstacles, persevering despite setbacks, developing their own procedures and equipment as they went along--those years were exhausting but also exhilarating. When Florey bumped into Dr. C. M. Fletcher, a former colleague, later in the war, he said:

> Those days were wonderful days, Fletcher. We--none of us can expect to know that kind of excitement again. That sort of thing can only happen once in anybody's lifetime.

Howard Florey was not unique. All Nobel laureates, whether in science, economics, literature, or peace, are universally marked by a passion for their work that comes close to obsession, a level of industry and application that are extraordinary, a near-total immersion in their field of endeavor, and a dedication that makes their work supremely fulfilling.

And this is the secret of their success.

References

Preface

"People keep writing to ask me": Denis Brian. *The Voice of Genius: Conversations with Nobel Scientists and Other Luminaries.* New York: Perseus Publishing, 1995, p. 142.

*How To Win The Nobel Prize.*Michael Bishop. *How to Win the Nobel Prize: An Unexpected Life in Science.* Cambridge, MA: Harvard University Press, 2003.

The Beginner's Guide. Peter Doherty, *The Beginner's Guide to Winning the Nobel Prize.* Columbia University Press, 2006.

"You too can win Nobel Prizes": Paul Berg and Maxine Singer. George Beadle, An Uncommon Farmer: The Emergence of Genetics in the 20th Century. Cold Spring Harbor NY: Cold Spring Harbor Laboratory Press, 2003, p. 245.

"If I knew what leads one": Interview with Neil Hollander, June 29, 2000. Nobel Voices Video History Project, 2000-2001. Smithsonian National Museum of American History.

"a bloody disaster": Doris Lessing, reported in Globe & Mail, May 12, 2008.

"one part to the person": http://nobelprize.org/alfrd/will/short _testamente.html.

"Occasionally a Laureate": Lena de Champs. Organizing the Nobel Festival Day—Some Recollections, June 21, 2000. http://nobelprize.org/nobelfoundation/history/dechamps/index.html
.

Chapter 1

"I found shelter": Mark Gozlan. "A Big Jump"; Mario Capecchi's Journey from Italian street kid to Nobel Laureate, Medscape Diabetes & Endocrinology, 2007. http://www.medscape.com/ viewarticle/564215_14

"I think I did learn": Mark Gozlan, 2007.

"No one who lives in the sunlight": quoted in Michael Dirda, *Book by Book: Notes on Reading and Life.* New York: Henry Holt, 2005, p. 22.

"All I maintain is": Albert Camus. *The Plague*. London: Penguin, 1960, p. 207.

"Mon cher enfant": Albert Camus. *The First Man*. New York: Vintage Books, 1995, p. 322.

"More characteristic of Nobel Prize winners": Harriet Zuckerman. *Scientific elite: Nobel laureates in the United States*. New York: Free Press, 1977.

"Why do my thoughts turn": Harry *Martinson. Cape Farewell*. London: Cresset Press, 1934, pp. 50-51.

"Unless you're poor": Arno Penzias in *Boston Globe*, February 5, 1989.

Chapter 2

"Family SES sets the stage": Selcuk R. Sirin. Socioeconomic Status and Academic Achievement: A meta-analytic review of research. *Review of Educational Research*, 75:3, 2005, pp. 417-453.

"They found few cases": A Rothenberg and G. Wyshak. *Family background and genius. Canadian Journal of Psychiatry*, 49:3, 2004, 185-191; Family background and genius II: Nobel Laureates in Science. *Canadian Journal of Psychiatry*, 50:14, 2005, 918-925.

"On my father's side": Maria Goeppert-Mayer. Nobel biography.
http://nobelprize.org/nobel_prizes/physics/laureates/1963/mayer-bio.html.

"Her results are compared": Harriet Zuckerman. *Scientific elite: Nobel laureates in the United States*. New York: Free Press, 1977.

"While my parents never had": Sheldon Glashow. Nobel Autobiography.   http://nobelprize.org/nobel_prizes/physics/laureates/1979/glashow-autobio.html.

"Probably the most important": Carl Wieman. Interview with Editor   of   Homeschool.com.
http://www.homeschool.com/articles/Nobel/default.asp.

Chapter 3

"What one really needs": George Wald, Letter to *Boston Globe*, 1980, on the subject of a Nobel sperm bank. Quoted in

Leslie Parrott, I Love You More, Grand Rapids, MI: Zondervan, 2001.

"Before they were in their teens": Mihaly Csikszentmihalyi. Creativity. New York: Harper Collins 1996.

"Some have theorized": Mihaly Csikszentmihalyi and Isabella Selega Csikszentmihalyi. Family influences of the development of giftedness. In *Ciba Foundation Symposium, The Origins and Development of High Ability.* Chichester UK: Wiley, 1993, pp. 187-206.

"he would have crushed me": Jean-Paul Sartre. *The Words.* New York: George Braziller, 1964, p.19.

"If potential confounding variables": Tennant, 1988, p. 1045.

"The relationship between scientific genius": W. R. Woodward, Scientific genius and the loss of a parent. *Science Studies*, 4, 1974, 265-277.

"One striking finding": Bernice T. Eiduson. *Scientists: Their Psychological World.* New York: Basic Books, 1962, p. 22.

"brings out clearly": S. M. Silverman. Parental loss and scientists. *Science Studies*, 4:3, 1974, 259-264, p. 263.

"A lot of the most talented people": Paul Greengard, Interview with Neil Hollander. Nobel Voices Video History Project 2000-2001. Smithsonian National Museum of American History.

"Work is the refuge": Quoted in Fritz Stern. *Five Germanies I have known.* New York: Farrar, Straus & Giroux, 2006, p. 68.

"We had the Encyclopaedia Britannica": Richard Feynman. *The Pleasure of Finding Things Out.* New York: Basic Books, 2000, pp. 3-4.

"At this point": Great Minds: Reflections of 111 Top Scientists by Balazs Hargittai, Magdolna Hargittai and Istvan Hargittai, 2014

Chapter 4

"had no degree: Baruch A. Shalev. 100 Years of Nobel Prizes. Los Angeles: The Americas Group, 3rd edition, 2005.

"John Gurdon" Nobel minds interview, 2012. Nobelminds.com

"Nearly 12 years of school": Winston Churchill. My Early Life. New York: Scribner, 1996, p. 38.

"I don't think I would have ever gotten" Lee Hartwell, Interview with Dr. Rochelle Esposito for the Lasker Foundation. http://www.laskerfoundation.org/learn/v_hartwell.htm

"It was Cambridge that made me": Georgina Ferry. Max Perutz and the Secret of Life. London: Chatto & Windus, 2007, p. 1.

"The Nobel Foundation": Nobel Laureates and Universities. http://nobelprize.org/nobel_prizes/lists/universities.html

"Cambridge University": Wikipedia, List of Nobel Laureates by University Affiliation.

"People keep e-mailing me": Quoted in Karen Heyman, David Baltimore's Redeeming Presidency. The Scientist, 17:8, 2003, 48.

"By the influence": Svante Arrhenius. *Worlds in the Making*. New York: Harper, 1908, p. 63.

"I have not the smallest molecule": quoted in Charles H. Townes, Making Waves. Woodbury NY: American Institute of Physics, 1995, p. 13.

"The energy produced": Ernest Rutherfordquoted in *New York Herald_Tribune*, September 12, 1933.

"All this stuff about traveling": Edward Purcell Lecture at Brookhaven National Laboratory in 1960. Quoted in obituary, *New York Times*, March 10, 1997.

"It really has an aura": Leon LedermanAcademy of Achievement Interview, June 27, 1992. http://www.achievement.org/auto doc/page/led0int-1

Chapter 5

Hitler's Gift: Jean Medawar and David Pyke. *Hitler's Gift*. New York: Arcade Publishing, 2001.

"I then remarked": Walter Gratzer. Eurekas and Euphorias: *The Oxford Book of Scientific Anecdotes*. New York: Oxford University Press, 2002, p. 189.

"To have been arrested": Max Perutz. *I Wish I'd Made You Angry Earlier: Essays on Science, Scientists, and Humanity*, Cold Spring Harbor, NY: Cold Spring Harbor Laboratory Press, 2003, p. 75.

"This leads me to my final": Max Perutz. *Is Science Necessary? Essays on Science and Scientists*. New York: Dutton, 1989, p. 201.

"No sum of money": D. Pyke. Contributions by German émigrés to British medical science. *QJM: An International Journal of Medicine*, 93, 2000, 487-495.

"A person, like myself": Walter Kohn, in UC Santa Barbara, *Daily Nexus*, January 17, 2001.

Chapter 6

"At least 178 Jews": http://www.jinfo.org/Nobel_Prizes.html.

"Harriet Zuckerman": Harriet Zuckerman, *Scientific Elite: Nobel Laureates in the United States*. New York: Free Press, 1977.

"Louise Sherby identified": Louise S. Sherby. *The Who's Who of Nobel Prize Winners 1901-2000*. Westport CT: Oryx Press, 2002 .

"Self-identified atheists": Baruch A. Shalev. *100 Years of Nobel Prizes*. Los Angeles: The Americas Group, 3rd edition, 2005.

"In science we have certain ways": Richard Aumann. Interview. Macroeconomic Dynamics, 9, 2005.

"After all my possessions": Shmuel Agnon. Nobel Acceptance Speech, December 10, 1966. http://nobelprize.org/nobel_prizes/literature/laureates/1966/agnon-speech.html.

"I don't believe in God": Albert Camus. Interview. *Le Monde*, August 31, 1956.

"Christianity may be OK": Matt Ridley. *Francis Crick: Discoverer of the Genetic Code*. New York: Atlas Books, 2006, p. 158.

"From religion comes": William Bragg,. Royal Institution Lectures, Christmas 1919. *The World of Sound*, 1920, pp. 195-196.

"I am absolutely, childishly, allergic": Interview in 1985. Quoted in Muge Galin, *Between East and West: Sufism in the novels of Doris Lessing*. Albany, NY: State University of New York Press, 1997, p. 54.

"I'm an atheist": Interview, *Paris Review* no. 88, Summer 1983, p. 35.

"Being an ordinary scientist": *Washington Times*, October 22, 2001.

"I think only an idiot" Christian Anfinsen quoted in Henry Margenau and Roy Varghese, Eds., *Cosmos, Bios, Theos:*

Scientists Reflect on Science, God, and the Origins of the Universe, Life, and Homo Sapiens. La Salle IL: Open Court, 1992, p. 139.

"I feel no need": Pearl Buck. *This I Believe*. Radio broadcast, 1951.

"My own view on religion": Bertrand Russell. *Why I am not a Christian*. New York: Simon & Schuster, 1957, p. 24.

"One of the great achievements": Steven Weinberg. *Facing Up: Science and its Cultural Adversaries*. Cambridge MA: Harvard University Press, 2001, p. 242.

"A spirit is manifest": Walter Isaacson. *Einstein: His Life and Universe*. New York: Simon and Schuster, 2007, p. 388.

"As a young doctor": Alexis Carrell. *The Voyage to Lourdes*. New York: Harper, 1950.

"Certain facts observed": Joseph T. Durkin. *Hope for our Time: Alexis Carrel on Man and Society*. New York: Harper and Row, 1965, p. 115.

Chapter 7

"Many of these women": Sharon Birtsch McGrayne. *Nobel Prize Women in Science: Their Lives, Struggles, and Momentous Discoveries*. Secaucus NJ: Citadel Press, 1998, p. 3.

"Wherever I went": Gertrude Elion. Interview, Academy of Achievement, March 6, 1991. http://www.achievement. org/autodoc/ page/eli0int-1

"Women, even now": McGrayne, 1998, p. 342.

"I can't think of anything": McGrayne, 1998, p. 353.

"As a matter of fact": Dorothy Hodgkin in BBC Radio interview, quoted in obituary by Max Perutz, *The Independent*, August 1, 1994.

"In 2004, women faculty": *Chronicle of Higher Education*, January 23, 2004.

"Compared with men": http://www8.nationalacademies.org/ onpinews/newsitem.aspx?RecordID=11741

"despite convincing evidence": J.S. Hyde, E. Fennema, and S. J., Lamon. Gender differences in mathematics performance: A Meta-Analysis. *Psychological Bulletin*, 1990, 107, 139-155.

"In graduate school": Henry Etzkowitz, Carol Kemelgor, and Brian Uzzi. *Athena unbound: The Advancement of Women in*

Science and Technology. Cambridge UK: Cambridge University Press, 2000, p. 210.

"If a student had a baby": Etzkowitz, Kemelgor, and Uzzi, 2000, p. 5.

"You can have it all!": McGrayne, 1998, p. 355.

"You have to make choices": Aung San Suu Kyi. *The Voice of Hope: Conversations with Alan Clements*, 1997, p. 184.

"I don't go anywhere": Interview, 1987. In Danille Taylor-Guthrie, Ed., *Conversations with Toni Morrison*. Jackson MS: University Press of Mississippi, 1994, p. 237.

Chapter 8

"Every single one of us": White House Press Conference February 9, 2012

"Among recent laureates": Tomas Lindahl, Nobel Banquet Speech, 2015; Arthur McDonald, Queen's Alumni Review, 4, 2015.

"The art of research": André Lwoff, quoted in Georgina Ferry. *Max Perutz and the Secret of Life.* London: Chatto & Windus, 2007, p. 26.

"All three of us": Rita Levi-Montalcini. Nobel autobiography. http://nobelprize.org/nobel_prizes/medicine/laureates/1986/levi-montalcini-autobio.html.

"It is striking that": Harriet Zuckerman. *Scientific Elite: Nobel Laureates in the United States.* New York: Free Press, 1977, p. 99.

"I can tell you how": Paul Samuelson. Nobel acceptance speech. http://nobelprize.org/nobel_prizes/economics/laureates/1970/samuelson-speech.html.

"If I ask myself": Hans Krebs, The making of a scientist, *Nature*, 215, 1967, 1441-1445.

"The most important event": Krebs, 1967, p. 1442.

"If you wish to become a scientist": Letter to Patrick Buckley, 1967. Hans Krebs, *Otto Warburg, Cell Physiologist, Biochemist, and Eccentric.* Oxford: Clarendon Press, 1981, p. 62.

"In their comparative youth": Zuckerman, 1977, pp. 241-242.

"Jim Watson was an amazing character": François Jacob. *The Statue Within.* Cold Spring Harbor NY: Cold Spring Harbor Laboratory Press, 1988, p. 264.

"If you hear about a scientist": *Curiosity is the Key to Discovery: The Story of How Nobel Laureates Entered the World of Science*. U.S. Department of Health and Human Services, 1992.

"every scientist can recall": Glenn Seaborg. *Adventures in the Atomic Age: From Watts to Washington*. New York: Farrar, Straus & Giroux, 2001, p. 13.

"I considered the surgeon's profession": Jacob, 1988, p. 92.

"Go off on vacation": Jacob, 1988, p. 213.

"From the moment I crossed": Jacob, 1988, p. 221.

"He treated his students": Mark Oliphant. *Rutherford: Recollections of the Cambridge Days*. London: Elsevier, 1972, p. 69.

"He drove us mercilessly": Oliphant, p. 108.

"Do not go to meetings": Shutsung Liao. Huggins, Charles Brenton. American National Biography Online, October 2002.

"Association with a leading teacher": H. A. Krebs. The Making of a Scientist. *Nature*, 215, September 30, 1967, 1442-1445, p. 1443.

"What you become in life": quoted in Allen L. Hammond, Ed., *A Passion to Know: 20 Profiles in Science*. New York: Scribner, 1984, p. 6.

"Don't be the best": Interview, Academy of Achievement, October 22, 1991. *http://www.achievement.org/autodoc/page/wat0int-1*.

"Dag Hammarskjöld was the most": Brian Urquhart. *Hammarskjöld*. New York: Norton, 1972, p. 320.

"There can be no better rule": Dag Hammarskjöld and the 21st Century, Dag Hammarskjöld lecture at Uppsala University September 6, 2001.

Chapter 9

"I think research and teaching": Roald Hoffmann. *The Scientist*, 14: 24, 10. December 11, 2000.

"A professor whose hands": quoted in Robert Marc Friedman, Balancing Act: The Historian as Playwright, lecture at Copenhagen and Beyond, Symposium in Copenhagen, September 1999, in *The Politics of Excellence: Behind the Nobel Prize in Science*. New York: Holt, 2001, p. 130.

"If you don't learn": Interview, Academy of Achievement, June 27, 1992. http://www.achievement.org/ autodoc/page/led0int-1.

"To teach, you really": Glen Seaborg. *Adventures in the Atomic Age: From Watts to Washington*, New York: Farrar, Straus & Giroux, 2001, p. 252.

"If you're worth your pay": Interview, *Region*, Federal Reserve Bank of Minneapolis, September 2002. http://www.minneapolisfed.org/publications_papers/pub_display.c fm?id=3399

"First figure out why": Richard Feynman. *Six Easy Pieces: Essentials of Physics Explained by its Most Brilliant Teacher*. New York: Basic Books, 2005, p. xx.

"Having students and working": Peter Kapitsa, Address at the Ioffe Physical-Technical Institute, 1968. *Experiment, Theory, Practice*. Boston: Kluwer, 1980, p. 222.

"The history of science": Recollections of Lord Rutherford, lecture delivered before the Royal Society May 17, 1966. In Jagdish Mehra, Ed., *The Physicist's Conception of Nature*. Boston, MA: D. Reidel Publishing Co., 1973, p. 750.

"Although I don't have a passion": Acceptance speech at Professor of the Year Award Ceremony at University of Colorado, 2004. http://www.colorado.edu/news/poy/wieman/wieman_acceptance.ht ml.

"I find that teaching": Richard Feynman. *All the Adventures of a Curious Character*, New York: Norton, 2005, p. 184.

"To teach and to love": Gabriela Mistral. *The Teacher's Prayer. Selected Poems of Gabriela Mistral*. Baltimore MD: Johns Hopkins Press, 1961, p. 225.

"There is no better way": George Paget Thomson. *J. J. Thomson and the Cavendish Laboratory in his Day*. London: Nelson, 1964, p. 171.

"Perhaps it was": Daniel C. Tsui. Nobel Autobiography, 1998. http://nobelprize.org/nobel_prizes/physics/laureates/1998/tsui-autobio.html.

"Only my pedagogic career": Czeslaw Milosz. Begining with my streets. New York: Farrar, Straus and Giroux, 1991, p. 97.

"I have come to believe": John Steinbeck. Like Captured *Fireflies*. *America and Americans and Selected Nonfiction*. New York: Penguin, 2002, p. 142.

"One thing that hasn't changed": Richard Taylor. *The Learning Team*, 4:4, June 1, 2001.

"I take teaching as seriously": http://www.math.buffalo.edu/~sww/ morrison/morrison_ toni-bio.html.

Chapter 10

"The popular mind": Michael Bishop. *How to Win the Nobel Prize: An Unexpected Life in Science*. Cambridge, MA: Harvard University Press, 2003, p. 61.

"The whole idea", Sydney Brenner *My Life in Science*, London: Biomed Central, 2001, p. 179.

"And yet it was": Eve Curie. *Madame Curie: A Biography*. Garden City NY: Doubleday, Doran & Co., 1938, p. 169.

"Everything is over": Curie 1938, p. 249.

"Work gives life": Susan Quinn. *Marie Curie: A Life*. Cambridge MA: Da Capo Press, 1996, p. 115.

"Between us we wove": François Jacob. *The Statue Within*. New York: Basic Books, 1988, pp. 307-308.

"You must be perfectly candid," Edward Edelson. *Francis Crick and James Watson: And the Building Blocks of Life*. Oxford: Oxford University Press, 1998, p. 225.

"The experience was magical": Daniel Kahneman Nobel autobiography. http://nobelprize.org/nobel_ prizes/economics/laureates/2002/kahneman-autobio.html. ©The Nobel Foundation 2002, used by permission.

"Our collaboration began": Carl Cori. Nobel Acceptance Speech, December 10, 1947. http://nobelprize.org/nobel_prizes/medicine/ laureates/1947/cori-cf-speech.html.

"The love for and dedication": Sharon Birtsch McGrayne. *Nobel Prize Women in Science: Their Lives, Struggles, and Momentous Discoveries*. Secaucus NJ: Citadel Press, 1998, p. 116.

"A hundred times every day": Quoted in Theodore C. Sorenson, *Kennedy*. New York: Harper and Row, 1965.

"Writing, at its best": Ernest Hemingway. Nobel Acceptance Speech, December 10, 1954. http://nobelprize.org/nobel_prizes/literature/laureates/1954/hemingway-speech.html.

"All I want to do": Olga S. Opfell. *The Lady Laureates: Women who have Won the Nobel Prize*. Lanham MD: Scarecrow Press, 1986, p. 54.

Chapter 11

"A steel mill": *California Monthly*, December 2001.

"A week in the lab":_*San Francisco Chronicle*, October 4, 2000.

"I would like to be a scientist": Harriet Zuckerman. *Scientific Elite: Nobel Laureates in the United States*. New Brunswick NJ: Transaction Publishers, 1996, p. 77.

"One day, a school teacher": Looking at Life with Gerard 't Hooft. Primenrich Plus, 18.

"You might have thought": quoted in *Seattle Post-Intelligencer*, October 5, 2004.

"I built a rocket": Horst Stormer. Nobel autobiography, 1998. http://nobelprize.org/nobel_prizes/physics/ laureates/1998/stormer-autobio.html.

"I think I was genetically": Stanford University News Service, October 16, 1996.

"Later statistics": Baruch A. Shalev. *100 Years of Nobel Prizes*. Los Angeles: The Americas Group, 3rd edition, 2005, p. 41.

"Two Russian researchers": V. N. Anisimov and A. I. Mikhal'skiĭ. Are Nobel prize winners getting older? Mathematical analysis of age and life span of the Nobel prize winners, 1901-2003. *Advances in Gerontology*, 15, 2004, 14-22. [Russian]

"Almost every important new discovery": quoted in Zuckerman. 1996, p. 164.

"Most of the progress": quoted in *Boston Globe*, December 10, 1982 .

"Age is, of course": quoted in James Gleick. *Genius: The Life and Science of Richard Feynman*. New York: Vintage, 1992, p. 347.

"The most precious": Leo Esaki. CIE/UTD Distinguished Lecture. Innovation and Evolution: Reflections on a Life in Research, University of Texas at Dallas, February 23, 2002.

"Malcolm Gladwell argues": Malcolm Gladwell. *Outliers: The Story of Success.* Boston: Little, Brown & Co., 2004.

"Never be the brightest": James Watson. *Avoid Boring People: Lessons from a Life in Science.* New York: Knopf, 2007, p. 114.

"To succeed in science": James Watson. Succeeding in Science: Some Rules of Thumb, 1993. In *A Passion for DNA: Genes, Genomes, and Society,* 2000, p. 124.

"When one gets older": Ralph W. Moss, *Free Radical: Albert Szent-Gyorgyi and the Battle over Vitamin C.* New York: Paragon, 1988, p. 196.

"I go to the lab": John B. Fenn, Interview with Margaret Warner, PBS, October 9, 2002.

"I can truthfully say": Selman Waksman. *My Life with the Microbes.* New York: Simon and Schuster, 1952.

"The chief rule": James Watson, Interview with Kelley Kawano, Random House, 2002. www.randomhouse.com/boldtype/0202/ watson/index.html.

"I often have the sense": James Watson. Dissemination of Unpublished Information, In *The Frontiers of Knowledge.* Garden City NY: Doubleday, 1975, p. 92.

"The year that Rutherford died": Peter Kapitsa, Recollections of Lord Rutherford, lecture delivered before the Royal Society 17 May 1966. In Jagdish Mehra, Ed., *The Physicist's Conception of Nature.* Boston, MA: D. Reidel Publishing Co., 1973, p. 765.

"Matthew Rablen and Andrew Oswald": Matthew D. Rablen and Andrew J. Oswald. Mortality and immortality: The Nobel Prize as an experiment into the effect of status upon longevity. *Journal of Health Economics,* 2008, 27:6, 1462-1471.

"UK Office for National Statistics": http://www.statistics.gov. uk/STATBASE/ssdataset.asp?vlnk=95   .

"Some people say": Charles Townes, Interview at University of California at Berkeley, June 17, 2005. UCBerkeley News. http://berkeley.edu/news/media/ releases/2005/06/17_townes.shtml.

"The moment you stop": quoted in Sharon Bertsch McGrayne, *Nobel Prize Women in Science: Their Lives, Struggles, and Momentous Discoveries*, 2001, p. 223.

"Retirement is the filthiest word": A. E. Hotchner, *Papa Hemingway: A Personal Memoir*. New York: Random House, 1966, p. 228.

"I am seeking to understand": quoted in Tyler Wasson, Ed., *Nobel Prize Winners*, 1987, p. 727.

Chapter 12

"The proportion of marriages": http://www. divorcerate.org. Also see Canwest News Report, 2010, http://www.canada.com/life/ Congratulations+divorc%C3%A9e/1713117/story.html

"For American billionaires": Mark Skousen, Forbes 400 Billionaires: 3 Lessons Investors can Learn from America's Richest People, October 3, 2006. http://www.investmentu.com/ IUEL/2006/20061003.html

"The divorce rate": Baruch A. Shalev. 100 Years of Nobel Prizes. Los Angeles: The Americas Group. 3rd edition, 2005.

"You should look around": Marc Abrahams, Nobel Thoughts: Linus Pauling. http://www.improb.com/ airchives/classical/nobel/pauling.html

"According to Jean Medawar": Jean Medawar and David Pyke. Hitler's Gift. New York: Arcade Publishing, 2001.

"A deal is a deal": *Boston Globe*, October 21, 1995.

Chapter 13

"Go out on a limb": Jimmy Carter. *The Virtues of Aging*. New York: Ballantine Books, 1998, p. 87.

"in the tradition of Alfred Nobel": Barry Marshall. Nobel Autobiography, 2005. http://nobelprize. org/nobel_prizes/medicine/laureates/ 2005/marshall-autobio.html

"function better as a single": Marshall, 2005.

"Was gastroenterology a science": Barry Marshall. *Helicobacter Pioneers: Firsthand Accounts from the Scientists who Discovered Helicobacters 1892-1982*. New York: Wiley, 2002, p. 181.

"We mixed up a complete": Barry Marshall. Academy of Achievement Interview, May 23, 1998. http://www.achievement.org/autodoc/ page/mar1int-6.

"There's a saying": Paul Lauterbur. Nobel Lecture, December 8, 2003. http://nobelprize.org/nobel_prizes/ medicine/laureates/2003/lauterbur-lecture.pdf.

"I always believed": Sydney Brenner. *My Life in Science*. London: Biomed Central, 2001, p. 106.

"When you have made": Annual Review of Physiology, 25, 1963.

"I feel like a village parson": Werner Forssmann in National Names Database. http://www.nndb.com/ people/706/000129319.

"Get out!": David Monagan & David Owen Williams. *Journey into the Heart: A Tale of Pioneering Doctors and their Race to Transform Cardiovascular Medicine*. New York: Gotham, 2007, p. 25.

"For years I was amazed": Werner Forssmann. *Experiments on Myself: Memoirs of a Surgeon in Germany*. New York: St. Martin's Press, 1972, p. 128.

"One may compare the art": Werner Forssmann. Nobel lecture, Dec. 11, 1956. http://nobelprize.org/nobel_prizes/medicine/laureates/1956/forssmann-lecture.html

"I think there should be a law": William H. Cropper, *Great Physicists: The Life and Times of Leading Physicists from Galileo to Hawking*. Oxford: Oxford University Press, 2004, p. 444.

"I think one could say": Allan L. Hammond, Ed., *A Passion to Know: 20 Profiles in Science*. New York: Scribner, 1984, p. 6.

"The peer review system": Anthony L. Peratt, Hannes Alfvén, www.tmgnow.com/repository/cosmology /AZlvarez.html.

"I'm convinced that": Luis Alvarez. *Alvarez: Adventures of a Physicist*, New York: Basic Books, 1987, p. 14.

"When an old and distinguished": Nobel address to university students in Stockholm, December 10, 1954. In Linus Pauling, *Linus Pauling in his own words: Selections from his Writings, Speeches, and Interviews*. New York: Touchstone, 1995.

"I have never been attacked": Hermann Hesse. *Reflections*. New York: Farrar, Straus and Giroux, 1974.

"catastrophe": James Knowlson. *Damned to Fame: The Life of Samuel Beckett.* London: Bloomsbury, 1996, p. 505.

"When you are in": Deidre Bair. *Samuel Beckett: A Biography.* New York: Harcourt Brace Jovanovich, 1988, p. 282 .

"Ever tried. Ever failed": Knowlson, 1996, p. 593.

"My parents provided": Roderick MacKinnon. Nobel Autobiography, 2003. http://nobelprize.org/nobel_prizes/chemistry/laureates/2003/mackinnon-autobio.html.

"If you develop a fascination": Roderick MacKinnon. Interview, Lasker Foundation, 1999. http://www.laskerfoundation.org/ wards/1999_b_interview_mackinnon.htm.

Chapter 14

"In scientific research": Sharon Bertsch McGrayne, *Nobel Prize Women in Science: Their Lives, Struggles, and Momentous Discoveries.* Secaucus NJ: Citadel Press, 1998, p. 211.

"All my life": Glen Seaborg. *Adventures in the Atomic Age: From Watts to Washington.* New York: Farrar, Straus and Giroux, 2001, p. 227.

"I don't know a great deal": Richard Feynman. *The Pleasure of Finding Things Out: The Best Short Works of Richard P. Feynman.* New York: Basic Books, 2005, p. 3.

"I have no special talents": letter to Carl Seelig, 11 March 1952. Alice Calaprice, Ed., *The Quotable Einstein*, 1996.

"You can't measure intelligence": Lillian Hoddeson and Vicki Daitch. *True Genius: The Life and Science of John Bardeen.* Washington: Joseph Henry Press, 2002, p. 273.

"The psychologist J. P. Guilford": J. P. Guilford. *The Nature of Human Intelligence.* New York: McGraw-Hill, 1967.

"Howard Gardner proposed": Howard Gardner. *Multiple Intelligences: New Horizons in Theory and Practice.* New York: Basic Books, 2006.

"after a certain point": Mihaly Csikszentmihalyi. Creativity. New York: Harper Collins, 1996, p. 259.

"is any act, idea": Csikszentmihalyi, 1996, p. 28.

"a genuinely creative": Csikszentmihalyi, 1996, p. 1.

"A new idea comes": Walter Isaacson. *Einstein: His Life and Universe.* New York: Simon and Schuster, 2007, p. 113.

"Too many kids in school": Interview with Joanna Rose, Stockholm, December 6, 2005.

"It was around this time": Ralph W. Moss, *Free Radical: Albert Szent-Gyorgyi and the Battle over Vitamin C*. New York: Paragon, 1988, p. 9.

"There are many situations" Eric Kandel. *In search of memory: The emergence of a new science of mind*. New York: Norton, 2006, p. 149.

"As we did our work": Ference Marton and Shirley Booth. *Learning and Awareness*. Mahwah, NJ: Lawrence Erlbaum, 1997, p. 154.

"I am not always right": Ference Marton, Peter Fensham, and Seth Chaiklin. A Nobel's eye view of scientific intuition: Discussions with the Nobel prize-winners in physics, chemistry and medicine (1970-86). *International Journal of Science Education*, 1994, 16:4, 457-473, p. 463.

"I consider that I have good intuition": Larisa V. Shavinina, Ed. *International Handbook on Innovation*. Atlanta, GA: Elsevier Science, 2003, p. 448.

"Csikszentmihalyi, in his study": Mihaly Csikszentmihalyi. *Creativity: Flow and the Psychology of Discovery and Invention*. New York: Harper Perennial, 1966.

"I have no particular intelligence": McGrayne, 1998, p. 213.

"usually happens at three": Leonard Lederman, at INTEL International Science and Engineering Fair, 2003.

"Practically all laureates": Marton, Fensham, and Chaiklin, 1994, p. 457.

"Poetry, I think": Interview, 1966. William Baer, Ed., *Conversations with Derek Walcott*. Jackson MS: University Press of Mississippi, 1996, p. 5.

"The hardest thing": Ernest Hemingway. Old Newsman Writes a Letter from Cuba. *Esquire*, December 1934. Quoted in Lisa Tyler, *Student Companion to Ernest Hemingway*. Westport, CT: Greenwood Press, 2001, p. 21

"Fiction, prose rather": Letter to Bernard Berenson September 24, 1954, in *Selected Letters 1917-1961*, 1981, p. 837.

"Seen from the outside": Joseph Brodsky. *On Grief and Reason*. New York: Farrar, Straus & Giroux, 1995, p. 300.

"I do not believe": Anatole France. *On Life and Letters*, second series. New York: Gabriel Wells, 1890, p. 214.

"I think poetry" Roald Hoffmann, interview, in Lewis Wolpert and Alison Richards, *Passionate Minds: The Inner World of Scientists*. New York: Oxford University Press, 1997, p. 23.

"He who has once seen": *King Solomon's Ring: New Light on Animal Ways*. New York: Routledge. 1949, p. 10.

"How does the idea": Walter Isaacson. *Einstein: His Life and Universe*, New York: Simon & Schuster, 2007, p. 549.

"Inspiration is not": Wislawa Szymborska. Nobel Lecture, December 7, 1996. http://nobelprize.org/nobel_prizes/literature/laureates/1996/szymborska-lecture.html.

"Surely, if those": Henri Dunant. *A Memory of Solferino (1862)*. Geneva: International Committee of the Red Cross, 1986. http://www.ourstory.info/library/1-roots/Dunant2/Solferino3.html.

"Late on the third day": Ann Cottrell Free. *Animals, Nature, and Albert Schweitzer*. Washington, DC: Flying Fox Press, 1982, p. 22.

Chapter 15

"When I ask myself": www.science.utah.edu /cronin.html, nd.

"Those whose work": Winston Churchill. *Painting as a Pastime*. New York: Cornerstone Library, 1965, p. 9.

"That one could live": François Jacob. *The Statue Within*. New York: Basic Books, 1988.

"Without passion": Theodore Mommsen. *History of Rome* (1908). New York: Routledge, 1996, p. 539.

"Try hard to find out": Joshua Lederberg, Interview with Lev Pevzner for Nobel Prize Internet Archive, March 20, 1996.

"To young people": Barry Marshall. Nobel Acceptance Speech, December 10, 2005. http://nobelprize.org/nobel_prizes/medicine/laureates/2005/marshall-speech.html.

"Work hard to find": Letter to Mike Flasar, November 9, 1966. Michelle Feynman, Ed. *Perfectly Reasonable Deviations from the Beaten Track: The Letters of Richard P. Feynman*. New York: Basic Books, 2005, p. 229.

"I had to work very hard": Rosalind Yalow, entry in *Current Biography Yearbook*, 1978, p. 460.

"You have to know": Interview, Academy of Achievement, June 27, 1992. http://www.achiev-ement.org/autodoc/page/led0int-1.

"I never thought of stopping": *Time Magazine*, October 24,1983.

"Passion, not planning": Barry Sharpless. *Nobel autobiography*, 2001. http://nobelprize.org/nobel_prizes/chemistry/laureates/2001/sharpless-autobio.html.

"Work. There is nothing else": Ronald W. Clark. *Einstein: The Life and Times*. New York: Harper, 1971, p. 338.

"Work is the only good thing": John Steinbeck. Notebook entry, 18 June 1938. *Working Days: The Journals of the Grapes of Wrath. New York: Penguin*, 1989, p. 38.

"To work was the only thing": Ernest Hemingway. *The Green Hills of Africa*. New York: Scribner, 1935, p. 72.

"For me writing": Pablo Neruda, Interview, *Paris Review*, no. 51, Spring 1971, p. 4.

"My life does not belong": Rigoberta Menchú Tum. I, Rigoberta Menchú: *An Indian Woman in Guatemala.* New York: Verso, 1984, p. 246.

"It does not seem to me": Kameshwar C. Wali, *Chandra: A Biography of S. Chadrasekhar*. Chicago: University of Chicago Press, 1991, p. 307.

Chapter 16
"What the future has": Albert Lutuli. *Let My People Go: An Autobiography*. New York: McGraw-Hill, 1962, p. 238.

"The tendency to see oneself": Albert Lutuli. *Let My People Go: An Autobiography*. New York: McGraw-Hill, 1962, p. 40.

"To remain neutral": Albert Lutuli. Nobel lecture, December 11, 1961. http://nobelprize.org/nobel_prizes/peace/laureates/1960/lutuli-lecture.html.

"The house was pervaded": Andrei Sakharov. Nobel Autobiography, 1975. http://nobelprize.org/nobel_prizes/peace/laureates/1975/sakharov-autobio.html.

"Progress, Peaceful Coexistence": Andrei Sakharov. *Thoughts on Progress, Peaceful Coexistence and Intellectual Freedom.* Petersham UK: Foreign Affairs Pub. Co., 1968.

"Yet, even so": Andrei Sakharov. Nobel Autobiography, 1975. http://nobelprize.org/nobel_ prizes/peace/laureates/1975/sakharov-autobio.html.

"Tomorrow there will be": quoted by John Polanyi in *Globe & Mail*, December 19, 1989.

"I have almost reached": Martin Luther King. *Why we Can't Wait*. New York: Harper & Row, 1964, pp. 87-88.

"I'm the son of a preacher": Irwin Abrams, *The Nobel Peace Prize and the Laureates*. Boston: G. K Hall & Co., 1988, p. 189.

"I have a dream": Martin Luther King. *I Have a Dream: Writings and Speeches that Changed the World*. San Francisco: Harper San Francisco, 1986, pp. 104-105.

"I don't know what": Gerold Frank. *An American Death*. Garden City NY: Doubleday,1972, p. 52.

"When I'm about to go": Iran Awakening—An Interview with Shirin Ebadi New America Media, May 20, 2006. http://news.newamericamedia.org/news/ view_article.html?article_id=8ad8e36442c10ef7fc33f0c8e70c08d8 .

"Instead of telling girls": News item in *Weekly Standard*, November 3, 2003. http://www.weeklystandard.com/Content/Public/Articles/000%5C 000%5C003%5C294whlna.asp.

"I had reached": Shirin Ebadi. *Iran Awakening: A Memoir of Revolution and Hope*. New York: Random House, 2006, p. xv.

"I feel afraid": Iran Awakening—An Interview with Shirin Ebadi, New America Media, May 20, 2006. http://news.newamerica media.org/news/view_article.html?article_id=8ad8e36442c10ef7fc 33f0c8e70c08d8.

Chapter 17

"Sometimes when I was starting": Ernest Hemingway. *A Moveable Feast.* New York: Scribner, 1964, p. 12.

"If you want fame": Richard Lingeman, *Sinclair Lewis: Rebel from Main Street*. Winnipeg, MB: Borealis Books, 2002, p. 451.

"I'd also say": Robert Franciosi, Ed., *Elie Wiesel: Conversations*. Jackson MS: University Press of Mississippi, 2002, p. 81.

"I have, despite": Acceptance speech for first Einstein Peace Prize, 1980. http://everything2.com/title/Alva+Myrdal

"Are there no other": Geoffrey Best. *Churchill: A Study in Greatness*. New York: Oxford University Press, 2002, p. 62.

"We have sustained": Winston S. Churchill. *Winston S. Churchill: His Complete Speeches 1897-1963*. (Ed., Robert Rhodes James). New York: Chelsea House, 1974, p. 6004.

"He said gravely": W. O. Thompson. *I Was Churchill's Shadow*. London: C. Johnson, 1981, p. 37.

"We shall not flag": Churchill, 1974, p. 6231.

"Never give in": speech at Harrow School on October 29, 1941. http://wiki.answers.com/Q/Who_did_Winston_Churchill_say_%7never_never_never_never_give_up%27_to

"Thus, then, on the night": Winston Churchill. *The Gathering Storm. History of the Second World War*, Vol. 1, Boston: Houghton Mifflin, 1948, pp. 666-667.

"Never flinch, never weary": *Winston S. Churchill: His Complete Speeches* 1974, p. 8633.

"I have one life": Jimmy Carter, Interview. *New York Times Magazine*, January 29, 1995.

"My wife has never": Jimmy Carter & Rosalynn Carter. *Everything to Gain: Making the Most of the Rest of your Life*. Fayetteville: University of Arkansas Press, 1987, p. 105.

"By far, my best years": Jimmy Carter. *Beyond the White House: Waging Peace, Fighting Disease, Building Hope*. New York: Simon & Schuster, 2007, p. xiii.

"The light has gone": Quoted in Wikipedia article. http://en.wikipedia.org/wiki/Theodore_Roosevelt.

"I wish to preach": Theodore Roosevelt. The Strenuous Life, Speech in Chicago April 10, 1899. http://www.theodore-roosevelt.com/trstrenlife.html.

"When I left the Presidency": *Theodore Roosevelt, An Autobiography*. New York: Macmillan, 1913, p. 602.

"I don't love life": Eugene O'Neill and Mark W. Estin. *Conversations with Eugene O'Neill*. Jackson, MS: University Press of Mississippi, 1990, p. 17.

"The tragedy of life": Mark W. Estrin, *Conversations with Eugene O'Neill*, University Press of Mississippi, 1990

"Born in a hotel room": A. Gelb & B. Gelb. *O'Neill*. New York: Harper, 1973, p. 939.

"a hair-raising picture": Edmund Wilson. *The Wound and the Bow*. Boston: Houghton Mifflin, 1941, p. 111.

Kipling, Rudyard. *Life's Handicap: Being Stories of Mine own People.* 1891. New York: Doubleday, Page, p. 167.

"Asia is not going": Rudyard Kipling. *The Letters of Rudyard Kipling*. Vol. 2, 1890-1899. New York: Macmillan, 1990, p. 376.

"Have you news": Rudyard Kipling. *Selected Poetry*. Ed., Craig Raine. Harmondsworth, UK: Penguin, 1992, p. 90.

"My son is named": Kinzaburu Oe. Quoted in *Princeton Weekly Bulletin*, 3 March 1997. http://www.princeton.edu/pr/pwb/97/0303/0303-oe.html.

"As a child": Kinzaburu Oe. Quoted in *Princeton Weekly Bulletin*, March 23,1997. http://www.princeton.edu/pr/pwb/97/0303/0303-oe.html.

"Losing an arm": Press release, University of Colorado, April 12, 2005.

Chapter 18

"I can say without affectation": Aleksandr Solzhenitsyn. *The Oak and the Calf: Sketches of Literary Life in the Soviet Union*. New York: Harper & Row, 1980, p. 272.

"Can a man who's warm": Aleksandr Solzhenitsyn. *One Day in the Life of Ivan Denisovich*. New York: Praeger, 1962 , p. 24.

"It was only when I lay": Aleksandr Solzhenitsyn. *The Gulag Archipelago 1918-1956: An experiment in literary Investigation*. New York: Harper & Row, vol. 2, 1974, p. 615.

"At the Novosibirsk": Solzhenitsyn. *The Gulag Archipelago 1918-1956: An experiment in literary Investigation*. New York: Harper & Row, vol. 1, 1973, p. 293.

"Live not by the lie": quoted in Ian Hunter. *Solzhenitsyn Left Enduring Legacy of Freedom. Catholic Register*, August 7, 2008.

"It is a fact": Menachem Begin. *White Nights: The Story of a Prisoner in Russia.* New York: Harper & Row, 1957, p. 48.

"No more war": quoted in http://www.upi.com/Audio/Year_in_Review/Events-of-1979/The-Carter-Administration/12311692377023-4.

"I was much cheered": Bertrand Russell. Portraits from Memory and Other Essays. London: G. Allen & Unwin, 1956, p. 30.

"I was still under interrogation": Wole Soyinka. Interview with Harry Kriesler, UC Berkeley, April 16. 1998. http://globetrotter.berkeley.edu/Elberg/Soyinka/soyinka-con0.html

"I know war": Amabel Williams-Ellis. *What was his Crime? The Case of Carl von Ossietzky.* London: Camelot Press, 1937, p. 6.

"It is fair to say": Wangari Maathai. *Unbowed: A Memoir.* New York: Anchor Books, 2006, p. 97.

"I have seen time": Maathai, 2006, p. 194.

"We are grateful": quoted in Daw, Aung San Suu Kyi , one of twenty great Asians http://www.burmalibrary.org/reg.burma/archives/199707/msg00100.html.

"It is not power": Aung San Suu Kyi. *Freedom from Fear and Other Writings.* New York: Penguin, 1991, p. 180.

"Saints, it has been said": Suu Kyi, 1991, p. 183.

"I have lived": Kim Dae-Jung. Nobel lecture, December 10, 2000. http://nobelprize.org/nobel_prizes/peace/laureates/2000/dae-jung-lecture.html.

"I have to say": Kim Dae-Jung. CNN Interview, June 15, 2001. http://archives.cnn.com/001/WORLD/asiapcf/east/06/15/koreakim.interview.

"I had no epiphany": Nelson Mandela. *Long Walk to Freedom: The Autobiography of Nelson Mandela.* Boston: Little, Brown, 1994, p. 95.

"During my lifetime": Nelson Mandela. "I am prepared to die." The History Place, Great Speeches Collection, n.d. http://www.history-place.com/speeches/ mandela.htm.

"A saint is a sinner": Anthony Sampson. *Mandela: The Authorized Biography*, New York: Vintage, 2000, p. 252.

"The time for the healing": Nelson Mandela. Inaugural Address as President of South Africa, May 10, 1994. http://www.wsu.edu:8080/~wldciv/world_civ_reader/world_civ_reader_/mandela.html.

"In spring 1942": Konrad Lorenz. Nobel autobiography, 1973. http://nobelprize.org/nobel_prizes/medicine/laureates/1973/lorenz-autobio.html.

"What does not kill me" Friedrich Nietsche. *Twilight of the idols, or, How to philosophize with a hammer.* Oxford: Oxford University Press, 2008, p. 2.

"All my major works": Jawaharlal Nehru: quoted in Book browse. http://www.bookbrowse.com/quotes/detail/index.cfm?quote_number=19

"In every human being's life": Aleksandr Solzhenitsyn. *The First Circle.* New York: Harper Collins, 1968, p. 288.

Chapter 19

Baruch Shalev estimates: Baruch A. Shalev. *100 Years of Nobel Prizes.* Los Angeles: The Americas Group. 3rd edition, 2005.

"excerpt from his trial": Ludmila Shtern. *Brodsky: A Personal Memoir.* Ft. Worth, TX: Baskerville Publishers, 2004, p. 142.

"They gave me terrible shots",Shtern, 2004, p. 153.

"The formula for prison": Joseph Brodsky. *Less than one: Selected Essays.* New York: Farrar, Straus & Giroux, 1986, p. 23.

"I'm the happiest": Joseph Brodsky. Quoted in Hoover Institution press release, September 27, 2000. http://www.hoover.org/pubaffairs/releases/_854911.html.

"At all costs": Joseph Brodsky. *On Grief and Reason.* New York: Farrar, Straus & Giroux, 1995, p. 144.

"My blood runs cold": Czeslaw Milosz, attributed.

"In the twentieth century": Czeslaw Milosz. Interview with Paul W. Rea 1987 Cynthia L. Haven, Ed., Czeslaw Milosz: Conversations. Jackson, MS: University Press of Mississippi, 2006, p. 89.

"To express the existential": Czeslaw Milosz. The art of poetry LXX. *Paris Review*, 133 (winter 94-95), 242-273, p. 242.

"Since I have lived": Czeslaw Milosz. Nobel Acceptance Speech. December 10, 1980. http://nobelprize.org/nobel_prizes/literature/laureates/1980/milosz-speech.html.

"Ah, but it is impossible" Parry, Albert. (Ed.) *Peter Kapitsa on Life and Science*. New York: Macmillan, 1968, p. 224.

"The moment even the greatest": Parry, 1968, p. 164.

"intensive physical labour": Gao Xingjian. *One Man's Bible*. New York: HarperCollins, 1999, p. 150.

"the most pernicious work": Gao Xingjian. Nobel biography, 2000.
http://nobelprize.org/nobel_prizes/literature/laureates/2000/gao-bio.html.

"I'm not involved": Gao Xingjian. Entry in everything2.com/title/Gao%25 0Xingjian.

"Literature is a place": Gao Xingjian. Literature as Testimony: The Search for Truth. In Horace Engdahl, (Ed.) *Witness Literature: Proceedings of the Nobel Centennial Symposium*, pp. 113-127. Hackensack, NJ: World Scientific, 2002, pp. 124-125.

"He said I was": http://www.signandsight.com/features/1910.html.

"Baruch Shalev analyzed": Baruch A. Shalev. *100 Years of Nobel Prizes*. Los Angeles: The Americas Group, 3rd edition, 2005.

Chapter 20

"I knew World War II": Ralph W. Moss, *Free Radical: Albert Szent-Gyorgyi and the Battle over Vitamin C*. New York: Paragon House, 1988, p. 100.

"Just as he reached": Moss, 1988, p. 140.

"Think boldly": Moss, 1988, p. 269.

"There was a story": Jeremy Bernstein, *Hans Bethe, Prophet of Energy*. New York. Basic Books, 1980, p. 79.

"A number of young men": Val Fitch. *The View from the Bottom. Chicago: Bulletin of the Atomic Scientists*, February 1974, 43-46, p. 45.

"I was fascinated": Renato Dulbecco. *Nobel Autobiography*, 1975. http://nobelprize.org/nobel_prizes/medicine/laureates/1975/dulbecco-autobio.html.

"Let's stop this": Renato Dulbecco. Interview for Oral History Project, Caltech, Pasadena CA, September 1988. http://oralhistories.library.caltech.edu/ 6/00/OH_Dulbecco_R.pdf.

"My unconquerable": Heinrich Böll. What's to Become of the Boy? New York: Penguin, 1981, p. 4.

"Art is always": Heinrich Böll. Nobel lecture, May 22, 1973. http://nobelprize.org/nobel_prizes/literature/laureates/1972/boll-lecture.html.

Chapter 21

"Never shall I forget": Wiesel, Elie. *Night*. New York: Hill & Wang, 1958, p. 34.

"The opposite of love": Wiesel, Elie. Quoted in *US News & World Report*, October 27,1986.

"I have endeavoured": Kertész, Imre. Nobel Acceptance Speech, December 10, 2002. http://nobelprize.org/nobel_prizes/literature/laure ates/2002/kertész-speech.html.

"I experienced my most radical": Kertész, Imre. Interview with Stefan Theil, *Newsweek International*, December 2002. http://isurvived.org/KertészINTERVIEW.html.

"Jews were required": Daniel Kahneman. Nobel autobiography, 2002. http://nobelprize.org/nobel_prizes/economics/laureates/2002kahneman-autobio.html.

"Above all, don't fear": Rita Levi-Montalcini http://blogs.america.gov/science/tag/viktor-hamburger.

Chapter 22

"When we asked": Csikszentmihalyi, Mihaly. Creativity. New York: Harper Collins 1996, p. 46.

"We were jolly lucky": *Newsday*, July 28, 2003.

"If you are lucky": Max Delbrück. Attributed.

"Success in research": A. L. Mackay. *A Dictionary of Scientific Quotations*. London: Institute of Physics Publishing, 1980, p. 80.

"It is better to be lucky": Ernest Hemingway. *The Old Man and the Sea*. New York: Scribner, 1952, p. 36.

"Do whatever you do": *Stanford Daily*, October 12, 2006.

"Ask good questions": INTEL International Science and Engineering Fair, 2003.

"Without luck, forget it": Leo Lederman. Academy of Achievement Interview, June 27, 1992. http://www.achievement.org/ autodoc/page/led0int-1.

"Fortune favors": Louis Pasteur, attributed.

Chapter 23

"When I was young": Alice Calaprice and Trevor Lipscomb. *Albert Einstein: A Biography.* Westport CT: Greenwood Press, 2005, p. 111.

"Potatoes": Helge Kragh, *Dirac: A Scientific Biography.* Cambridge UK: Cambridge University Press, 1990, p. 73.

"Of all physicists": William H. Cropper. *Great Physicists: The Life and Times of Leading Physicists from Galileo to Hawking.* New York: Oxford University Press, 2001, p. 375.

"No! I have nothing": Abraham Pais. *The Genius of Science: A Portrait Gallery.* New York: Oxford University Press, 2000, p. 70.

"Almost instantly": Kary Mullis. *Dancing Naked in the Mind Field.* New York: Vintage, 1998, p. 19.

"Eventually it moved": Mullis, 1998, p. 21.

"As Yogi Berra": István Hargittai, *Candid Science II: Conversations with Famous Biomedical Scientists.* Hackensack NJ: World Scientific Publishing Co., 2002.

"Some people eat too much": Mullis, 1998, p. 139.

Chapter 24

"A bloody disaster": Globe & Mail, May 12, 2008.

"The Nobel is a ticket": T. S. Eliot, attributed.

"Kiss of death" quoted in Ewa Czarnecka and Aleksander Fiut, *Conversations with Czeslaw Milosz.* New York: Harcourt Brace Jovanovich, 1981, p.97.

"The Prize is very good": *István Hargittai, The Road to Stockholm*: Nobel Prizes, Science and Scientists. New York: Oxford University Press, 2002, p. 5.

"If you're not careful": *Napa Register*, March 25, 2001.

"Oh, no, I was afraid": The Harvard Guide, http://www.news.harvard.edu/guide/faculty/fac8.html].

"This is the end of me": Richard Lingeman, *Sinclair Lewis: Rebel from Main Street.* New York: Random House, 2002, p. 354.

"In any case": Newsweek, October 16, 1978.

"If you love science": Sharon Birtsch McGrayne. *Nobel Prize Women in Science: Their Lives, Struggles, and Momentous Discoveries*. Secaucus NJ: Citadel Press, 1998, p. 200.

"like being hit": *Los Angeles Times*, October 9, 1998.

"I have always declined": Letter to Nobel Foundation refusing the Prize, October 1964.

committee turned him down: http://infao5501.ag5.mpi-sb.mpg.de:8080/topx/archive?link=Wikipedia-Lip6-2/16340.xml&style#5.

"Immensely thankful": Robert Conquest, *Courage of Genius: The Pasternak Affair*. London: Collins & Harvill, 1961, p. 90.

"a purely political act": Conquest, 1961, p. 78.

"Considering the meaning": Conquest, 1961, pp. 92-93.

According to Tolstoy: *Washington Post* January 29, 2007.

"This account has been disputed": https://www.stanford.edu/dept/slavic/cgi-bin/?q=node/288.

"My mother died": PBS On-Line News Hour, October 11, 2000.

Chapter 25

"Ligate pancreatic ducts": Michael Bliss, Banting: *A Biography*. Toronto: University of Toronto Press, 1984, p. 53.

"Never was there a time": Bliss, 1984, p. 295.

"If there is even": W. Pierce. *Air War, its psychological, technical and social implications*. New York: Modern Age Books, 1939, p. 181.

"A scientist belongs": Morris Goran, The Present-day Significance of Fritz Haber, *American Scientist*, 35:3, July 1947, pp. 400-403, 306. http://www.soils.wisc.edu/~barak/soilscience326/haber_amsci.htm

"I tender my resignation": Patricia Rife. *Lise Meitner and the Dawn of the Nuclear Age*. Boston: Burkhauser, 2006, p. 114.

"The life's work": Letter to Richard Willstatter December 1933. Dietrich Stoltzenberg, *Fritz Haber: Chemist, Nobel Laureate, German, Jew*. Philadelphia PA: Chemical Heritage Foundation, 2004, p. 209.

"the whole school": New York Times, February 27, 2009.

"Hitler "was a warrior"": http://en.wikipedia.org/wiki/Knut_Hamsun%_7s_obituary_of_Adolf_Hitler.

"A study of 10,365 lobotomies": Bengt Janssen, Controversial psychosurgery resulted in a Nobel Prize. http://nobelprize.org/nobel_prizes/medicine/articles/moniz/index.html.

"All the great masterful races": Naval War College Address, June 2, 1897. http://www.theodore-roosevelt.com/tr1898.html

Chapter 26

"in countless of his works": Kjell Espmark. *The Nobel Prize in Literature: A study of the criteria behind the choices*. Boston: G. K. Hall & Co., 1986, p. 17.

"It saved me": Lyle Larson, The Nobel Prize for Literature, http://homepage.smc.edu/larsen_lyle/nobel_prize_for_literature.htm.

"Graham Greene will receive": Michael Sheldon, *Graham Greene, The man within*. London: Heinemann, 1994, p. 421.

"At the mercy of": Espmark, 1986, p. 67.

Chapter 27

"Part of being a scientist": Leon Lederman, quoted in New York Times, October 20, 1988

"I know that I'll write": Interview, Paris Review, no. 116, Fall 1990.

"As with other creative endeavors": Arthur Kornberg. *For the Love of Enzymes: The Odyssey of a Biochemist*. Cambridge, MA: Harvard University Press, 1989, p. 298.

"I was awed by enzymes": Arthur Kornberg Remembering our Teachers. *Journal of Biological Chemistry*, 276:1, January 2001. http://www.jbc.org/content/276/1/3.full?maxtoshow=&HITS=10&hits=10&RESULTFORMAT=&searchid=1&FIRSTINDEX=70&rcsourcetype=HWCIT

"I can imagine no life": Stanford Moore Papers, Rockefeller University.

"I dreamed of finding": I. P. Pavlov. Autobiography, in *Selected Works*. Honolulu HI: University Press of the Pacific, 1955.

"Fellow students": William H. Fowler. Nobel Acceptance Speech, December 10, 1983.

http://nobelprize.org/nobel_prizes/physics/laureates/1983/fowler-speech.html.

"One has to live it": Interview at Meeting of Nobel Prize winners, Lindau, Germany, December 12, 2000.

"I always say": Obituary, *The Independent*, March 12, 2007.

"thanked his parents": MacDiarmid, Alan. Nobel lecture, December 8, 2000. http://nobelprize.org/nobel_prizes/chemistry/laureates/2000/macdiarmid-lecture.html.

"I am a very lucky person": MacDiarmid Alan. Nobel Autobiography, 2000. http://nobelprize.org/nobel_prizes/chemistry/laureates/2000/macdiarmid-autobio.html.

"Those days were wonderful": Lennard Bickel. *Rise up to Life: A Biography of Howard Walter Florey who Gave Penicillin to the World*. New York: Charles Scribner's Sons, 1972 , p. 222.

``I have trained more than 200 students`` Robert Lefkowitz, Nobel Banquet speech, December 10,. 2012

"The journey has been": Richard Langworth. *Churchill by Himself: The Definitive Collection of Quotations*. London: Ebury Publishing, 1965, p. 20.

Index

58388157R00110

Made in the USA
Charleston, SC
09 July 2016